The Land of
POCO TIEMPO

The Land of
POCO TIEMPO

Charles F. Lummis

ILLUSTRATED FACSIMILE EDITION

The University of New Mexico Press

ALBUQUERQUE

Library of Congress Catalog Card No. 66-22698
1966 edition

MANUFACTURED IN THE UNITED STATES OF AMERICA
BY THE UNIVERSITY OF NEW MEXICO PRINTING PLANT
ALBUQUERQUE, NEW MEXICO

56853

Foreword to the 1952 Edition

TWANGING HIS GUITAR, Charles Fletcher Lummis, seated a little higher than the group of scientists, writers, and Indians squatted on the ground encircling a bonfire of cedar and piñon, was singing—not one of the Indian or Spanish songs of which he had recorded hundreds—but Kipling's "Mandalay." It was thus, under the stars of the New Mexico sky, that I first met the noted author, explorer, archaeologist, historian, builder, and journalist. It was during the 1910 summer session of the School of American Research in the Rito de los Frijoles Canyon of the Pajarito Plateau. Lummis was at the apogee of his fame, nationally and internationally. Writing in the department titled "In the Lion's Den" in his magazine *Out West,* he had been a vehement pleader for Indian rights. He had become the successful protagonist of enterprises for the preservation of American antiquities and landmarks, including the historic missions of California. He had won the friendship and support of Theodore Roosevelt and his coterie of zealous conservationists for his altruistic undertakings and organizations. The books of Lummis had found acceptance by leading Eastern publishers. His reputation as an author, historian, and ethnologist was firmly established.

Born and reared in Massachusetts, Lummis had matriculated in the Harvard class of 1881. While a student he had published *Birchbark Poems*, a little volume of nature verse. He had traversed on foot the length and

breadth of New England. Truly, he was a disciple of the
outdoor school of Thoreau and Burroughs.

In 1882, at the age of twenty-three, he turned westward. For two years he worked on a newspaper in Ohio.
It was in 1884 that he walked 3,507 miles in 143 days,
starting out from Cincinnati, and after roundabout ways
through New Mexico and Arizona, reached the Pacific
at Los Angeles. There he joined with others in 1885 to
establish a daily newspaper. He was its city editor for
three years. As such he often worked twenty hours out
of twenty-four, fighting political gangsterism, cleaning up
what was then a typical, rowdy, Western frontier community rapidly outgrowing its provincialism.

Due to overwork and strenuous living, Lummis suffered a stroke, a brain clot, which paralyzed his left side,
making his left arm useless, impeding his speech, and
forcing him to abandon his position on the Los Angeles
Times.

With brave resolve, Lummis entered deliberately upon
a second phase of his adult existence, a career of adven-
ture which was punctuated by repeated attacks upon his
life and which included living with the Penitentes in an
isolated New Mexico plaza at the foot of Mount Taylor,
distant from railroad and urban comforts. Finally came
his adoption by the Tigua pueblo of Isleta, south of Albuquerque, where he became as one of the Indians. All
these years he was fighting with stubborn will to regain
his physical health. He tells the story graphically in his
autobiographical booket *My Friend Will*, at the same time
disclosing his thoughts and beliefs about life, death, God,
and immortality. It was during these years he wrote many
of his feature articles and verses for magazines and newspapers, which later were embodied to a certain extent and
in revised form in his books, climaxed by *The Land of
Poco Tiempo.*

During this period he met Adolph F. Bandelier, in whose companionship Lummis blossomed into a full-fledged American archaeologist. Together, on foot and on horse- and burroback, they explored the Pueblo world, particularly the fastnesses of the Pajarito Plateau west of Santa Fe. "Thousands of miles of wilderness and desert we trudged side by side," wrote Lummis; "camped, starved, shivered, learned and were glad together. . . . My big camera and glass plates in the knapsack on my back, the heavy tripod under my arms, up and down pathless cliffs, through tangled canyons, fording icy streams and ankle-deep sands, we travailed; no blankets, overcoats or other shelter; and the only commissary a few cakes of sweet chocolate and a small sack of parched pop-corn meal." He took thousands of photographs which today are a historic treasure trove. He boasted, writing of himself in the third person: "His physique was as hard as his head. He was hardly five feet seven inches, but sinewy and agile as a panther, and of really extraordinary strength. All over his body the knots and strands of muscles stood out like whipcords. . . . He stripped 135 pounds." Lummis followed Bandelier into Peru and Bolivia. To test his recovery to health and strength he climbed the 19,000-foot volcano, El Misti, above Arequipa, in Peru. In reading the record, one seems to be aware of secret envy by Bandelier of the Lummis prowess and success as an author, while on the other hand, Lummis probably sought to emulate Bandelier as an archaeologist and Spanish historian. Be that as it may, Lummis, dressed in Spanish bolero jacket, corduroy trousers, a colored kerchief knotted about his head, as I first saw him in the Rito camp, was an unforgettable figure.

Lummis was primarily a journalist, a columnist and feature writer with a newspaperman's zest, "this hunger in the head," as he styled it, to find out for himself the inwardness of happenings and the why and wherefore of things. He asserted that he never had been found to state as fact that which could be proved false. This zest for knowledge led him into fields of science, the writing of historic books, the founding of noted institutions such as the School of American Research, of which he was one of the incorporators, to friendships at home and abroad and fellowship with men like Hewett, Hodge, Springer, and presidents of colleges and universities. He enjoyed discussions and delighted in polemic, of which latter he was a master.

His last years were spent in California, in the house he had built with his own hands with stones out of the Arroyo Seco. Surrounded by family, neighborhood friends, admirers, and many visitors eminent in music, drama, science, and literature, from near and far, he dug up some of his earlier manuscripts which had not found favor with publishers and sent them out once more in the hope that they would find acceptance, as some of them did. He grew roses and water lilies, fed the birds and squirrels which had made their home on the large sycamore tree at his door step. He continued to plan earnestly the organization and perpetuation of the Southwest Museum in Los Angeles, with its Lummis tower, a monument to his lifework and ambitions. Blindness overtook him, but nevertheless he compiled his poems of earlier years and had the satisfaction of holding in his hands the finished volume of *The Bronco Pegasus* just before he passed away. Even in the years of his retirement he continued to dictate a column for the Los Angeles Sunday *Times,* his newspaper love of more than forty years; a newspaper man to the last!

From both literary and scientific standpoints, *The Land of Poco Tiempo* is Lummis' most important book. In it he embodied episodes that went to the very essence of the character of the people who inhabited the Southwest. Their customs, religion, songs and ceremonies, traditions, history, and their outlook upon environment and life, pass in review in colorful detail. The Indians, as well as the descendants of the Spanish Conquistadores and the Anglo pioneers, are the actors on a stage of titanic proportions and overwhelming grandeur of scenery. Wrote Lummis in 1918, ten years before his death, "I never can write about anything that I don't personally know or haven't exhaustively dug up." Lummis never wrote an unclean book; his English is crystal clear without a trace of pedantry. His passages descriptive of ancient ruins, New Mexico missions, and Indian ceremonies are classics. *Poco Tiempo,* when it first appeared in 1884, aroused the interest not only of the traveling public, but also of writers, painters, scientists, to whom the volume disclosed an inexhaustible vein of subjects for pen, brush, and research. They took to heart in increasing numbers the slogan first sounded by Lummis, "See America First!" The book also established the reputation of Lummis as an author whose writings were sought by magazines, newspapers, and book publishers. The book is as up-to-date today as it was then. Whenever I am asked, as I am occasionally: "If I have time for only one book on the Southwest, which do you recommend?" I reply invariably: "By all means read Lummis' *The Land of Poco Tiempo!*"

PAUL A. F. WALTER

Santa Fe, New Mexico
May 5, 1952

THE LAND OF POCO TIEMPO

SUN, SILENCE, AND ADOBE.

THE

LAND OF POCO TIEMPO

BY

CHARLES F. LUMMIS

ILLUSTRATED

NEW YORK

CHARLES SCRIBNER'S SONS

1928

To

EVA AND DOROTHEA

CONTENTS

CONTENTS

VIII

LIST OF ILLUSTRATIONS

[FROM PHOTOGRAPHS BY THE AUTHOR.]

THE LAND OF POCO TIEMPO

THE LAND OF POCO TIEMPO

SUN, silence, and adobe—that is New Mexico in three words. If a fourth were to be added, it need be only to clinch the three. It is the Great American Mystery—the National Rip Van Winkle— the United States which is *not* United States. Here is the land of *poco tiempo*—the home of " Pretty Soon.' Why hurry with the hurrying world? The " Pretty Soon " of New Spain is better than the " Now! Now !" of the haggard States. The opiate sun soothes to rest, the adobe is made to lean against, the hush of day-long noon would not be broken. Let us not hasten —*mañana* will do. Better still, *pasado mañana*.

New Mexico is the anomaly of the Republic. It is a century older in European civilization than the rest, and several centuries older still in a happier semi-civilization of its own. It had its little walled cities of stone before Columbus had grandparents-to-be ; and it has them yet. The most incredible pioneering the world has ever seen overran it with the zeal of a prairie-fire three hundred and fifty years ago ; and the embers of that unparalleled blaze of exploration are not quite dead to-day. The most superhuman marches, the most awful privations, the most devoted heroism, the most unsleeping vigilance wrested this

bare, brown land to the world ; and having wrested
it, went to sleep. The winning was the wakefullest
in history—the after-nap eternal. It never has wak-
ened—one does not know that it ever can. Nature
herself does little but sleep, here. A few semi-
bustling American towns wart the Territorial map.
It is pockmarked with cattle-ranches and mines,
where Experience has wielded his costly birch over
millionaire pupils from the East and from abroad.
But the virus never reached the blood—the pits are
only skin-deep. The Saxon excrescences are already
asleep too. The cowboy is a broken idol. He no
longer " shoots up the town," nor riddles heels reluc-
tant for the dance. His day is done ; and so is that
of the argonaut. They both are with us, but their
lids are heavy. And around them is New Spain
again, dreamy as ever after their rude but short-lived
nudging. The sheep—which feed New Mexico—
doze again on the mesas, no longer routed by their
long-horned foes ; and where sheep are, is rest. The
brown or gray adobe hamlets of the descendants of
those fiery souls who wreaked here a commonwealth
before the Saxon fairly knew there was a New
World ; the strange terraced towns of the aboriginal
pioneers who out-Spaniarded the Spaniards by unknown centuries ; the scant leaven of incongruous
American brick—all are under the spell. And the
abrupt mountains, the echoing, rock-walled cañons,
the sunburnt mesas, the streams bankrupt by their
own shylock sands, the gaunt, brown, treeless plains,
the ardent sky, all harmonize with unearthly unanimity.

" Picturesque " is a tame word for it. It is a picture, a romance, a dream, all in one. It is our one corner that is the sun's very own. Here he has had his way, and no discrepancy mars his work. It is a land of quaint, swart faces, of Oriental dress and un-spelled speech; a land where distance is lost, and the eye is a liar; a land of ineffable lights and sudden shadows; of polytheism and superstition, where the rattlesnake is a demigod, and the cigarette a means of grace, and where Christians mangle and crucify themselves—the heart of Africa beating against the ribs of the Rockies.

There are three typical races in New Mexico now —for it would be wrong to include the ten per cent. "American" interpolation as a type. With them I have here nothing to do. They are potential, but not picturesque. Besides them and around them are the real autocthones, a quaint ethnologic trio. First, the nine thousand Pueblo Indians—peaceful, fixed, house-dwelling and home-loving tillers of the soil; good Catholics in the churches they have builded with a patience infinite as that of the Pyramids; good pagans everywhere else. Then the ten thousand Navajo Indians—whose other ten thousand is in Ari-zona — sullen, nomad, horse-loving, horse-stealing, horse-living vagrants of the saddle; pagans first, last, and all the time, and inventors of the mother-in-law joke gray centuries before the civilized world awoke to it. Last of all, the Mexicans; in-bred and isola-tion-shrunken descendants of the Castilian world-finders; living almost as much against the house as in it; ignorant as slaves, and more courteous than kings; poor as Lazarus, and more hospitable than Crœsus; Catholics from A to Izzard, except when they take occasion to be Penitentes—and even then fighting to bring their matted scourges and bloody crosses into the church which bars its door to them. The Navajos have neither houses nor towns; the Pueblos have nineteen compact little " cities; " and the Mexicans several hundred villages, a part of which are shared by the invader. The few towns of undiluted gringo hardly count in summing up the Territory of three hundred by four hundred miles.

If New Mexico lacks the concentration of natural picturesqueness to be found elsewhere, it makes up in universality. There are almost no waterfalls, and not a river worthy of the name. Cañons are rare, and inferior to those of Colorado and the farther Southwest. The mountains are largely skyward miles of savage rock; and forests are far between. But every landscape is characteristic, and even beautiful—with a weird, unearthly beauty, treacherous as the flowers of its cacti. Most of New Mexico. most of the year, is an indescribable harmony in browns and grays, over which the enchanted light of its blue skies casts an eternal spell. Its very rocks are unique —only Arizona shares those astounding freaks of form and color carved by the scant rains and more liberal winds of immemorial centuries, and towering across the bare land like the milestones of forgotten giants. The line of huge buttes of blood-red sandstone which stretches from Mt. San Mateo to the Little Colorado, including the " Navajo Church " and a thousand minor wonders, is typically New Mexican. The Navajo Reservation—which lies part in this Territory and part in Arizona—is remarkably picturesque throughout, with its broad plains hemmed by giant mesas split with wild cañons. So are the regions about Jemez, Cochití, Taos, Santa Fé, Acoma, and a few others.

The most unique pictures in new Mexico are to be found among its unique Pueblos. Their quaint terraced architecture is the most remarkable on the continent; and there is none more picturesque in the world. It remains intact only in the remoter pueblos —those along the Rio Grande have been largely Mexicanized into one-storied tameness. Laguna, on the Atlantic & Pacific Railroad, has some three-story terraced houses still. Acoma, on its dizzy island-cliff, twenty miles southwest, is all three-storied; and Taos, in its lovely, lonely valley far to the north, is two great pyramid-tenements of six stories.

And the Pueblos—they are picturesque anywhere and always, but particularly in their dances, races, and other ceremonials. These are Indians who are neither poor nor naked; Indians who feed themselves, and ask no favors of Washington; Indians who have been at peace for two centuries, and fixed residents for perhaps a millennium; Indians who were farmers and irrigators and six-story-house builders before a New World had been beaten through the thick skull of the Old; Indians who do not make pack-beasts of their squaws—and who have not "squaws," save in the vocabulary of less-bred barbarians. They had nearly a hundred republics in America centuries before *the* American Republic was conceived; and they have maintained their ancient democracy through all the ages, unshamed by the corruption of a voter, the blot of a defalcation or malfeasance in office. They are, under the solemn pledge of our Government in the treaty of Guadalupe Hidalgo, citizens; and are the most flagrantly wronged in our country.   Their numerous sacred dances are by far the most picturesque sights in America, and the least viewed by Americans, who never found anything more striking abroad. The mythology of Greece and Rome is less than

A PUEBLO CLOTHO SPINNING IN THE SUN.

theirs in complicated comprehensiveness, and they are a more interesting ethnologic study than the tribes of inner Africa, and less known of by their white countrymen.

The flat Mexican towns themselves are picturesque —for the ardent sun of the Southwest makes even an adobe beautiful when it can pick it out in violent antitheses of light and shade. Their people—ragged courtiers, unlettered diplomats—are fast losing their pictorial possibilities. The queue and the knee-breeches, the home-woven poncho, with a hole in the centre whereby the owner may thrust his head through the roof of his combined umbrella and over-coat, are passed or passing away ; and in their place have come the atrocities of the Hebrew clo'man. But the faces—they are New Spain still.

New Mexico, like the dearest women, cannot be adequately photographed. One can reproduce the features, but not the expression—the landmarks, but not the wondrous light which is to the bare South-west the soul that glorifies a plain face. The positive is an enchantment, the *negative* a disappointment. One cannot focus upon sunlight and silence; and without them the adobe is a clod. Description of the atmospheric effects of the Southwest is the most hopeless wall against which language ever butted its ineffectual head. "The light that never was on sea or land" spends itself upon the adobe and the chap-paro. Under that ineffable alchemy of the sky, mud turns ethereal, and the desert is a revelation. It is Egypt, with every rock a sphinx, every peak a pyra-mid.

Life is the least vital feature of New Mexico. The present is a husk—the past was a romance and a glory. The Saxon invasion which came with the railroad has reacted almost to syncope. It is in lit-tle hope of revivification until the settlement of land titles shall be effected, and a national shame of forty years effaced. The native, stirred to unwonted per-spiration by the one-time advent of the prodigal *peso,* has dropped back to ease with dignity—dignity in rags, mayhap, but always dignity. To the old ways he has not wholly returned—just to the old joy of living, the broad content of sitting and remembering that one has lungs for this ozone and eyes for this day-dream. I would not be understood that it is idle-ness. There is work; but such unfatal work! The *paisano* has learned to live even while he works—wherein he is more wise than we, who slave away youth (which is life) in chasing that which we are past enjoyment of when we overtake it. He tills his fields and tends his herds; but there is no unseemly haste, no self-tripping race for wealth. *Lo que puede* —that which can be—is enough. It needs not to plough deep, nor to dun the land with fertilizers. The land has taken it easy, too, and after three cen-turies of uncrowded fruition appears not exhausted, but restful and conservative. Why urge it? There will be enough! The river's roily pulse circulates in ten thousand *acequias*, and gives drink to the thirsty fields, cupped with their little irrigating-beds. Its sediment is fertilizer sufficient. So shall the brown bean, the quenchless chile, the corn and the wheat, fill the store-room—and what need of more?

If the Neo-Mexicanized Saxon were as minded to spiritual graphicism as the un-Saxonized New Mexi-can, he would have one chief fetich in the territory of his adoption—the burro. That devoluted donkey is the sole canonizable type of northern New Spain —the genius of the adobe. He works—as New Spain works — faithfully but without friction. He dreams, meanwhile, as New Spain dreams—ruminat-ing on dignity and wisdom; by the wall to the sun

in winter, by the wall to the shade in summer.   Here
he is not an ass, but a sage.   The tatters of a myriad
cockle - burs fray not his ease—*he* can *afford* rags.
He is slow, but more sure than the End.   He humps
his load up dizzy heights where a chamois might have
vertigo.   He rolls down a precipice a few hundred
feet, alights upon his pack, and returns upon his way
rejoicing—grateful for exercise without exertion.   He
likes life and life likes him.   I never saw a dead burro, save from undue confidence in railways—which
have been the death of many worse citizens.   He
rouses now and then in the dead watches of the
night to sing about it.   The philosopher who has a
few lifetimes to spare might well devote one to the
study of the burro.   He is an honorable member of
the body social and politic.   Indeed, he is the corner-
stone of New Mexico.   Without him civilization
would have died out.   He ambles cheerfully in such
burdens that one doubts if chemical analysis may not
be necessary to determine the presence of burro in
the mass ; and in such solution or at ease he is perfectly content.

The house to which the burro is natural comple-
ment is worthy as he.   The adobe is the easiest
made and the most habitable of dwellings.   It is cool
in heat, and warm against utter cold.   As for its
making, one merely flays one's lawn, stands the epi-
dermis on edge, and roofs it.   There is the house—
and as for lawn, a bare one is as good as one with
cuticle.   The unadulterated adobe is a box, boarded
of sods two feet long, eight inches wide, four inches
thick, cut, turned over, and left to dry out ; then laid
upon one another in a mortar of their own mud ;

floored with clay, roofed with peeled pine - trunks
crossed with branches that are in turn thatched with
hay, and that buried under a foot of gravel.

From that the adobe mounts up by easy degrees

THE CARRÊTA.

to any elegance.   Its possibilities are endless.   Charming residences, creditable four-story blocks, are
equally facile to the adaptive " mud brick."   It moves
at ease in the prouder society of brick and stone, and
teaches them new manners which are far from un-
couth.

The bone of New Mexican industry is unchanged, but new ways have tattooed the skin. The plough-share of a pine-stub, the phaeton with half-ton wheels of wood, and their frontier associates have yielded to steel and iron. The *carreta* is no longer a familiar institution. To find it one must go to the utter hamlets, where the shriek of its ungreased wheels—hewn cross-sections of a giant sycamore—still affrights the drowsy land. There are even a few threshing-machines; but most of the people are content to be no better than the Scripture, and thresh with quadrupedal flails. Within the limits of the territorial capital, the bean and the shock of wheat are trodden out to this day by scurrying hoofs. The mission grape still pays its ruddy juice to the importunity of bare feet and tireless knees. The sickle is king of the harvest field; and the pasture is three hundred miles square.

Business methods are conservative amid the elder population. Witness the following true story:

Cristobal Nuñez and Transito Baca are two venerable residents of Llanito, brothers-in-law, and equally addicted to legitimately obtained hiccoughs. Having amassed a few round *pesos* by labor at a sheep-shearing, they formed a partnership, bought ten gallons of whiskey in Santa Fé, and started over mountainous roads to retail it in outlying *plazas* from a small cart. Each knowing the other's failing, they swore a solemn oath that neither would give the other a drop during the trip; and thus forearmed, they set out. They had spent every cent, save a nickel which Cristobal had accidentally retained.

"*Valgame Dios!*" groaned Cristobal, after they

had gone a few miles, "but it is very long without to drink. For the love of the Virgin, *cuñado*, give me a little to me."

"But how! That thou not rememberest our compromise?" asked the virtuous Transito.

Cristobal groaned again, and rode a few miles in silence. Then an idea percolated through his shaggy locks—the nickel in his pocket.

"It is truth, *compadre*, that we compromised not to give us not one drop. But of the *to sell* was nothing said. See! That I have *cinco centavos!* Sell-me a drinklet to me."

"'*Sta bueno!*" said Transito, pocketing the nickel and pouring his companion a small dose. "The saints are witnesses that I kept my oath. I give not, but sell."

Everything takes its time in New Mexico; but in half an hour the inspiration got across the wagon to Transito.

"*Carrambas!* How buy not *I* a drinklet *tambien?* *I* have *cinco centavos* now. Sell-me a little to me, *compadre*." And Cristobal did so, thereby regaining his nickel.

"But wait-me a so-little, and I will buy a drinklet from thee also, that we may drink joined."

Back went the nickel to Transito; and in a moment the two old men were clinking glasses mutually "*á la vuestra salud, compadre.*" This seemed more social, till a disturbing thought occurred to Transito.

"*Pero hombre!* Thou hast had two drinks and I only one. Go, sell-me to me another, that we are equals."

This logic was not to be gainsaid; and Cristobal

doled out the whiskey and resumed the nimble coin. Just then a trace broke.

"Ill-said horses! And of ill-said fathers and mothers! That now we have to go to camp here. To-morrow we will fix the harness."

But they did not fix it to-morrow, nor the next day, nor the next. They just stayed in camp and attended strictly to business—which was remarkably good. Now Cristobal was merchant, and Transito customer; and now *al contrario*. No one else came along to disturb the routine of trade, until the third day, when a sheep-herder found two white-headed men sleeping beside an empty ten-gallon keg. A much-worn nickel lay in one half-closed fist, and the wool-propeller took it along for luck.

"And how to you went the journey?" people asked in Llanito.

"*Mala suerte,*" sighed Cristobal, sadly. "We sold all our whiskey; but some *ladron* robbed to us asleep of all we had taken in."

Mines there are, but no monumental ones. The stories of ancient and wonderfully rich Spanish mines in the Southwest are unmitigated myths, every one. The placers of the Real de Dolores date only from 1828, and nuggets are still washed out there with primitive rocker and pan. There is not, and never has been, a hydraulic mine in New Mexico, despite the enormous areas of placer-ground. As for the mines in rock, they do not count here, for they are purely Saxon institutions, and have in no wise affected the native life of New Spain. The most important of our mines, ethnologically, is the ancient "Great Turquoise," in the round, gray crown of "Mount"

Chalchuitl—a hoary knob seven thousand feet above the sea-level, and seventy above its own base. This was the only prehistoric mine in the Southwest; and the veins and nuggets of green and rarer blue through its chalky heart were worked with the stone hammer before Columbus and before gunpowder. Its output made a dim commercial link between the buffalo-robe of Dakota and the parrot-plume of Yucatan. The mine is viewed with awe by the sporadic tourist as the tomb of a few hundred Pueblo Indians imprisoned at hard labor by those cruel Spaniards, and caved upon by the more merciful rocks. That is a characteristic invention of the Saxon enemy. The Spaniard invariably treated the aborigine better than we did; he never made an Indian work in a mine in New Mexico; and he never worked the Great Turquoise—which, in turn, never caved upon anyone. The only significance the mine had was as the supplier of a substance prized by all Indians, and hence as a promoter of distrustful intercourse between the near Pueblos who controlled it and their more or less distant neighbors, none of them knowing gold until the Conquest, and none having use for it even yet. A few absolutely perfect turquoises have been mined there by Americans; but the game was never worth the fuse.

Society is little bitten with the unrest of civilization. The old ways are still the best ways; and the increasing reprobates who would improve upon their fathers are eyed askance. The social system is patriarchal, and in many degrees beautiful. Mexican and Pueblo children are, as a class, the best-mannered, the most obedient, the least quarrelsome in

America. Respect for age is the corner-stone of society. A son, untouched by our refining influence,
would as soon put his hand in the fire as smoke before his parents—even though he have already given
them grand - children. A stranger, be he poor or
princely, is master of the house to which he shall
come. It may be the veriest hut of a *jacal* amid the
farther ranges; it may contain but a single crust of
bread and a sheepskin upon the clay floor; but house
and crust and couch are his, though his hosts sleep
supperless upon the bare adobe—and all with a high,
gentle courtesy that palaces might study. The An-
glo-Saxon is not born to intrinsic hospitality, and can
understand its real meaning as little as anything else
one has to *learn*. He promulgates the Brotherhood
of Man; but to him man *means* his brothers, and not
his fifty-ninth cousins. It is partly because of this
that he disavows, and is infested with, the tramp.
Hospitality is as Latin in fact as in name. It is in
the blood; and outside that blood it is not. In the
old days, one might zigzag the whole incomparable
area of Spanish America, without money or letters,
with no introduction beyond his patent of humanity,
and be assured everywhere of a "welcome to your
own house, Señor." It is very much so to-day, and
the traveller in the outer darkness will meet a hospitality as utter as he shall find the lack of it in the few
"civilized" communities along his way. There are
some Mexicans and some Pueblos who have learned
in bitterness to shut their doors upon the hospitality-
robber of late years; but they are very few. Almost
every Spanish home in New Mexico is a home too
for the wayfarer; and in the pueblos it is the sacred

office of the Cacique to see that no stranger is un-
cared for.   There are poor people among both peoples—fewer in the Indian ranks—but no Mexican and
no Pueblo since time began ever went hungry, unless
lost in the wilderness ; and none ever suffered for the
necessaries of life, and none was ever outcast of his
kind.   One or two Pueblos in a generation, and several Mexicans in a week, go behind the bars ; but if the
Southwest were peppered with poor-houses, no soul
of either race would ever be found therein.   To Saxons
who are associable, both peoples are the kindliest, the
most thoughtful, and the least meddlesome of neighbors.

The Mexican is popularly listed—thanks to the
safely remote pens of those who know him from a car
window, and who would run from his gray wrath—
as cowardly and treacherous.   He is neither.   The
sixth generation is too soon to turn coward the blood
which made the noblest record of lonely heroism that
time ever read.   As for treachery, it is merely a question of philosophy whether, in exterminating a rattlesnake, we shall invite it to strike us first, that it may
have "a fair show."   The Latin method is *not* to
allow the foe the privilege of the first bite—which is
sense if not chivalry, and the code of Christian warfare if not of the duello.   And on the other hand,
there is as great a ratio of absolute "chivalry," and of
giving one's self the disadvantage in favor of a worthy
foe, among Mexicans as among the Superior Race.

As the burro is the spiritual type of the Southwest,
so is the sheep the material symbol.   He rendered the
Territory possible for three centuries, in the face of
the most savage and interminable Indian wars that
any part of our country ever knew.   He fed and

clothed New Spain, and made its customs, if not its laws. He reorganized society, led the fashions, caused the only machinery that was in New Mexico in three hundred years, made of a race of nomad savages the foremost of blanket-weavers, and invented a slavery which is unto this day in despite of the Emancipation Proclamation. The first sheep that touched what is now United States came to New Mexico with Coronado in 1540; but they did not last. Half a century later, Oñate brought the merino flocks whose descendants remain. The modest wool-bearer soon came to the front. He was the one available utilization of New Mexico. Society gradually fell apart into two classes—sheep-owners and sheep-tenders. One man at the beginning of this century had two million head of sheep, and kept twenty-seven hundred peons always in the field with them, besides the thousands more who were directly dependent. That was the Spanish governor Baca. "El Guero"* Chaves, the first governor of New Mexico under the Mexican Republic, had a million sheep. The last of the great sheep-kings, Don José Leandro Perea, of Bernalillo, died a few years ago leaving two hundred thousand. Since his time, the largest flocks range from eighty thousand to one hundred and ten thousand ; and there are more than a dozen individual holdings of over fifty thousand head.

The social effects of such a system, wherein four-fifths of the Caucasian male population were servants at five to eight dollars a month to a handful of mighty *amos*, are not far to trace. The most conscientious of these frontier czars had perforce a power beside which

* The Blonde.

the government was a nonentity; and the unscrupulous swelled their authority to an unparalleled extent. It was easy to get a few hundred poor shepherds into one's debt; and once in, the *amo*, with the aid of complaisant laws, took good care that they should never get out. He was thenceforth entitled to the labor of their bodies—even to the labor of their children. They were his *peons*—slaves without the expense of purchase. And peonage in disguise is still effective in New Mexico.

Sheep made commerce, too. There were no railroads, and hence no markets. The wool was of necessity consumed at home. In the cumbrous Mexican looms it grew into invincible carpets and perennial garments. It was practically the only material of wear, save the Indian buckskin. Every Mexican woman wore a head-shawl, and every man a blanket, both home-woven. The surplus went into blankets for "export." Every March a representative from every Spanish family in New Mexico joined the annual *conducta* at the rendezvous below Socorro, with his flintlock in the crook of his elbow, his burros laden with the winter's weaving and a little hoard of coffee, popcorn-meal, and dried meat. Thus secure in numbers against the incessant Apache, the mercantile army marched down the Rio Grande and overran Sonora; trading its staples, to the "fool Sonoreños" of its weaving-songs,* for brazil-wood, silks, cattle,

---

* The weaver sitting at his loom was wont to sing,

> " *Tejo te, y no te tejo—*
> *Que eres por un*
> *Sonoreño pendejo.*"

"I weave thee, and I weave thee not, that art for a Sonoran fool." It was a frank confession—*these* blankets were very shabbily woven.

oranges, coffee, dried-fruits, and Indian girls. This caravan was gone out of New Mexico from March to September. Then the traders turned hunters, and sallied out in force to the vast eastward plains to kill and jerk the year's supply of buffalo-meat. After that long and perilous trespass on the lands of the centaur Comanches, came the expedition to the salt-lakes of Zuñi for the year's salt; and by the time the horses were rested from that arduous march, it was the season for starting on another *conducta*.

Wool was not an unmixed blessing to the New Mexican lover. It was his bread and butter, but also the excuse for a curious hardship. Every New Mexican Rachel had a Rachel's father, and Jacob's lot was multitudinously hard. Matches were not trusted to heaven, but made sure by parental hands. Having elected a son-in-law prospective, the first concern was to prove him. In return for the proposed honor of admitting him to the family, the *padre politico* demanded his services as representative in the *conducta ;* then in the bison-hunt; then in the salt-harvest. Having been thus arduously and dangerously employed for a year without material reward, the lover might receive the girl, or he might get the squashes. It is but a few years since a young Mexican friend was mittened with a gift of *las calabasas.* If the match was still on, however, the suitor had still one important social agendum before betrothal—the presentation of an Indian girl to his dulcinea for a hand-maiden. As Indian girls ruled steady in the Sonora market at about five hundred dollars—which was several times more money than most young *paisanos* ever saw—the only resort of the average lover was to

PUEBLO GIRL WINNOWING BEANS.

organize a band of similarly circumstanced **friends,**
take the war-path against the marauding Apaches **or**
Navajos, find an encampment, slay the **warriors, and**

bring the females home captive—or go themselves to the land where are neither rigorous fathers-in-law nor *calabasas*.

The railroad swept away all this a decade ago, bringing the world's markets to the corral-side, and making the *conducta* a thing of the past. But sheep remain as much the life of the Territory as in the old days. A commercial aberration once led trusting souls to plant cattle on the plateaus of New Mexico; and as the fever grew, Scottish lords and Holland bankers absorbed counties and became cattle-kings. The counties, in turn, absorbed banks and baronies; and very little remains to show, save costly maps promulgating gaudy steamers plying upon lithographic rivers, where in fact a minnow must stand upon his head to keep his gills wet. For three years and more the railroads in New Mexico have been largely a procession of cattle bound for Kansas and other States of corn and water, until a vast majority of the great herds has been shipped; and the sheep lords it again over his own. New Mexico was made for him and not for steers; and he has come out first-best in the costly contest with those who would have revised nature.

There is, perhaps, no essential kinship between sheep and superstition; but here at least the twain are next-door neighbors. In this simple, restful, patriarchal, long-lonely world, the chief concerns of life are the field, the flock, and—the warding-off of witches. The entire Indian population believes in them to a soul; and "They who have the Evil Road" are a daily menace to every aboriginal community. The prime duty of the numerous medicine-

men of each tribe and village is to keep down witchcraft and punish witches; and the faith figures in
every phase of the infinitely complicated superstitio-
religion of these thirty thousand New Mexicans.   Of
the fourfold more numerous Mexican population, the
assertion cannot be quite as sweeping, for there are
many educated families; but probably full sixty per
cent. of the whole people are as firm believers in
witchcraft; and every undiluted Mexican hamlet has
its suspected *brujas*.   They are even in Santa Fé.
The judicial history of the Territory abounds in
formal witchcraft trials; and summary executions
extra legem had not wholly ceased among the Mexicans half a decade ago; while among all the Indian
races such punishments are still of full force and
judicial form.

Cumulative penitence is a deep-rooted custom of
both races.   With the Indians, the tribal vicars
mortify the flesh in behalf of their people, but almost
solely by excessive fasts.   Among the Mexicans still
survives that astounding perversion of the once-
godly Franciscan Third Order, the Penitentes, but
now confined to a few remote hamlets.   These fanatics do penance. for themselves only, and in Lent
achieve their sin-washing for the year.   They flay
their bare backs with plaited scourges, wallow naked
in beds of cactus, bear crushing crosses, and on Good
Friday actually crucify one of their order, chosen to
that supreme honor by lot.   This is not all of the
past.   The Penitente crucifixions had not missed a
year up to 1891.   Hundreds of Americans have
witnessed this ghastly passion-reality; and I have
had the privilege of photographing it.

With the superstitions dwells the simple folk-lore.
That of the Mexicans is scant; but that of the
Indians infinite and remarkably poetic. And both
races have great store of folk-songs—composed by
Those of Old, or by lonely shepherds.

These are but fugitive glimpses of the Land of
Pretty Soon. A picture of sharp outline and definite
detail would better diagraph some of the contents of
New Mexico, but it would not be a true picture of the
country. Landscape and life are impressionist, and
will submit neither to photography nor to figures.
Years of study and travel do not itemize the picture—
there still remain in the memory but a soft, sweet
haze of shifting light and shade, a wilderness of
happy silence, an ether of contentful ease, wherein
we live and die and are glad.

THE GENIUS OF THE ADOBE.

II

"LO" WHO IS NOT POOR

"LO" WHO IS NOT POOR

HAD the hunchbacked sermonizer in pentameter acquired residence in the American Southwest, the language would be poorer by one phrase which was once rather witty, and is still staple. He would have found Indians who built houses four stories taller than did their Caucasian neighbors; who had as much land per capita, and tilled it as effectively; who wore upon the average as good clothing, and, upon occasions of state, better—among whom, in fact, poverty is quite unknown—and we should have heard nothing of " Lo, the poor Indian." For the Pueblo, the most striking ethnologic figure in our America to-day, is emphatically an Indian who is not poor from any point of view. Physically, mentally, morally, socially, politically, he need not shun comparison with the average of his lately acquired countrymen; and he even affords luxuries to which the superior race has not yet risen. As an Indian he is a paradox; as a human, he is unique in the whole world. He is the one racial man who enjoys two religions, irreconcilable yet reconciled; two currencies, millenniums apart in the world's ripening; two sets of tools, as far asunder as the Stone Age from the locomotive; two sets of laws, one coeval with Confucius, and the other with the Supreme Court;

two languages that preceded us; and two names, whereof the one we hear was ratified by the sacrament of Christian baptism, while the other, whereby he goes among his own, was sealed upon his infant lips with the spittle of a swart godfather at a pagan feast. He is the sole aborigine on earth who inhabits many-storied buildings, and the only man who ever achieved, in our land, such architecture of unburnt clay. He is a hereditary and immemorial farmer, who learned neither architecture nor agriculture from us, but gave us our first lessons in that which is a fundament of farming in an area equal to twenty-

TIGUA YOUTH, ISLETA.

five per cent. of our whole country—irrigation. From whichsoever side we view him, he is worthy a comprehension which has never been publicly had of him.

Our genuine understanding of the Pueblo dates from the new school of American archæology, of which Bandelier (with the early guidance of Lewis H. Morgan) was founder and is head. I make this statement advisedly ; for science is by little the richer for the peckings of others at this field. The essential errors of research in our Southwest were two : first, the employment of students, or rather detectives, limited severely to recording details which were weighed and collated solely by men who never saw the field, and who therefore had not the necessary horizon. And second, entire disregard of all the documentary and geographical accessories, without which such research is absolutely blind. There have been a few genuine students, but they are unfortunately as rare as genuine. As to the armchair archæologists, they do not count.

The very traditions of history have been rudely sent to the right-about face in the last decade, for a new school in history * also has arisen. Bandelier has been the first American historian fully to employ the three essential factors of history—record, physical geography, and ethnology, That these *are* history, and that history cannot be without them, has been long established ; but the theory went long lonely.

To the uninitiated, the general mode in which the history of Spanish America has been "studied" is little short of incredible. The student has seemed actually afraid that he might be biased by knowledge —by seeing the country and the peoples which have made that history, or by consulting the vast mass of reliable Spanish record, and has at all events avoided both "dangers." As example of this strange self-blinding, I may mention the long current dispute as to the respective ages of Santa Fé (actually founded

---

* Headed by the greatest of American historians, living or dead, Francis Parkman ; and that brave apostle of truth and clarity, John Fiske.

in 1605) and St. Augustine (actually founded in
1560).   But the closest historian has had his day.
It is now even deemed necessary to consult the recorded facts, though they are in another language;
and to have at least seen the races and the geography,
which are equally important factors.

Since Morgan so completely exploded the romantic
school of history, we hear no more of the "emperor-
ship" of Montezuma, nor of his vast "treasures;" of
Cabeza de Vaca's discovery of New Mexico; of Aztec
and Toltec ruins within the United States.   Those
shibboleths of an ignorance which was too lazy or too
lame to go to walk and see, have been expurgated
from the vocabularies of science, and remain only to
the unconscious humorists who study ethnology from
a flying Pullman or an Eastern closet.

It is a matter of knowledge, at last, that Cabeza de
Vaca never saw New Mexico.   The tireless, fearless
Franciscan fraile, Marcos of Nizza, first found the territory, and first saw its distinctive aborigines.   That
was in 1539.   A year later he brought face to face
with the Pueblos the first Caucasian soldier they had
ever seen—the neglected Coronado.   Thence on,
Spanish knowledge of the Pueblos was practically
continuous and progressively accurate; and by the
time the Saxon had raised his first hut in the New
World, these Indians were vassals of Spain and con-
verts of Rome.   Both in justice to history, and for the
comprehension of the present, it is proper to reiterate
here that the Spanish never enslaved the Pueblos;
never made them work in mines; found no mines in
New Mexico and made none; never forced the Indians
to abandon their old religion and adopt the new.

Spain's was the most comprehensive, humane, and effective "Indian policy" ever framed. In all three qualities it surpassed all the Indian policies of all other European nations and the later United States rolled into one.

The sedentary population of the Southwest was never great. The closet-historian puts it at from two hundred thousand upward; but it is now positively established that it never exceeded thirty thousand in historic times, if ever. There are in New Mexico alone the ruins of hundreds upon hundreds of stone pueblos; but the fact which has been overlooked is that they were not all occupied at once. They were the successive homes of a small race, which, though "sedentary," moved and took its seat along almost as readily as May-day pilgrims change flats in New York. The circumambient savage became too attentive; or drouth prevailed; or an epidemic came; or lightning befell the *estufa;* or any one of a thousand other omens indexed the will of The Trues, and forthwith the aborigine changed his town and his farm to a new place, and left the bones of the old to befool undreamed-of theorizers. His numbers are practically the same as three hundred years ago. Then he counted, in New Mexico, about nine thousand, and about nine thousand he counts to-day. This is in keeping with a very notable and seldom noted truth of history. Wherever our ancestors, the Earth-hungry, have touched America for more than a century, the aborigine is practically extinct.* In the

---

* The last census shows 250,000 Indians remaining in the United States. Ninety per cent. of these are in the area which we absolutely had not touched a century ago. And over one-third are in the area guarded and preserved by the Spanish.

far greater American area covered by Spain for three
centuries and a half, the aborigine is practically as
numerous as at the Conquest, and much better off.
When this unquestionable fact becomes more widely
recognized, we shall hear less of " Spanish atrocities "
in the New World.

The Pueblo is neither Aztec nor Toltec.   No one
who uses the latter word can defensibly define it ;
and as to the Aztecs, they are merely the Nahuatl,
who still dwell about the lake of Mexico.   The
Pueblo has no connection with them, further than
that he has learned a few Aztec words brought to
him by the Spanish.   All the ruins in our Southwest
are purely Pueblo ruins, and there is not an Aztec
stone among them.

A pet illumination, also, of the same now exploded
romancing, was to catalogue the Pueblo as patiently
awaiting the second coming of Montezuma.   The
Pueblo has no concern with Montezuma, and never
did have ; and at the fable and those who would put
it in his mouth, he simply laughs.   The truth is, that
this myth was invented in Mexico by Mexicans in
1846 as a campaign document to lead the Pueblos
into political combinations.   It was industriously
propagated here, but utterly failed to be swallowed
by the Indians, and never imposed on anyone until
the usual closet-archæologist came along to adopt it,
since when it has flourished for want of contradiction.

Racially the Pueblo is a palpable Mongol.   He
even finds, often, the same inter-slipperiness of *l* and
r.   It is not essential, however, to infer his migration
from China *via* the Northwest—though the Navajo,
his nomad prodigal son, speaks still the tongue of

the great Tin-neh tribe of Alaska, and is himself called
Tin-neh by the Pueblos.   But migration has ceased
to be our only ethnologic alternative since "equivalent development" was thought out.

When history found the Pueblo he dwelt in houses
like his own of to-day, tilled his farms by irrigation

INTERIOR OF A PUEBLO HOUSE.   (ISLETA.)

as now, and lived in general by most of his present
rules.   Of him we have far fuller and more accurate
historic record than of any other aborigine within our
borders; and as he changed slowly wherein he
changed at all, the picture holds largely good for the
remoter past.   At the Conquest he had no brute servants—neither beast of burden, watch-beast, milker,

nor meat-giver. In this the Apache of the Plains
was ahead of him, for *he* had vehicle and pack-animal
—the sledge and the Eskimo dog. The only domestic animal of the Pueblo was the turkey; and it
was kept rather for its feathers than for its meat.
The Pueblo crops were corn, squashes, beans, and,
in places, cotton. Spain gave him, and America at
large, the horse, cow, sheep, goat, ass, cat, and dog.
These he assimilated with an industry proportionate
to their value to him ; and of them all he now has
enough. Every male Pueblo, in effect, has a horse,
and most have burros. Sheep have supplanted cotton, and the processes of the farm are carried on with
modern implements. An Indian of Isleta has recently
purchased even a threshing-machine, and several
principales in various pueblos own buggies, while
nearly every family has a good farm-wagon.

The first effect of the Spanish Conquest was a
unique racial stride. The Pueblo, who never knew
any metal before, despite the fables of his gold, passed
at one step from the stone age to the age of iron,
copper, and silver; from sole man to man with the
beasts in his employ. He was given, and promptly
adopted, wheat and fruits, which have since become
an integral part of his economy. Grapes he was
given about 1630, and in 1891 he made a round
thousand barrels of wine in the one pueblo of Isleta,
besides selling thousands of dollars' worth of fruit.
Wine is made also in the pueblos of Jemez and
Sandia; but practically in none of the rest.

In 1540 the Pueblo dressed in garments of cotton,
buckskin, robes of twisted rabbit - hides, tunics of
yucca fibre, and mantles of feathers. He already

knew how to tan, spin, and weave, to make handsome
baskets, and an excellent semi-glazed pottery, without the potter's wheel. With no tools but stone he
worked, broadly speaking, as well as we with steel,
because time was nothing. That most of these things
are not so well done by him to-day is *not* a sign of
decadence, but rather of evolution. He has found
more profitable outlets for his time. He taught the
Navajo to weave, and now the Navajo is his weaver,
while he takes that leisure for his improved and more
exacting farm. Blankets are no more made by the
Pueblos ; and they of Moqui alone continue to weave
the women's dresses, with which they supply all the
other pueblos, as they do also with baskets. The
only weaving still common to all the towns is that of
the *fajas*, or bright-hued girdles, and their smaller
counterparts for garters and queue-fastenings. These
are woven exclusively by the women now ; and nothing is left, save at Moqui, of the ancient custom under
which the textile art pertained exclusively to the men.
Isleta makes hardly any pottery, having found it better to buy the indispensable water-jars from villages
which have smaller agricultural cares. The Pueblo is
not entirely dull in such matters. He was a prehistoric trader. He had an established commerce in salt
(from his several extensive salines), tanned buffalo-
hides and buckskin, turquoise, mineral paint, and cotton mantles. He traded not only with his brethren,
but with Apache, Comanche, Navajo, and Ute ; with
tribes from eastern Kansas to northern Mexico.
None was too savage to be customer ; and having
traded with his visitors by day, he shut them out by
night, and slept with his hand on his scalp and every

house-top patrolled.   His commercial instinct was
not repressed by the Conquest, which rather gave
him a new market and greater safety in the old ones.
To-day his income from the towns of the Hlah-fáh-
deh amounts to tens of thousands of dollars annually.
He meanders by express-train or burro-train from
Santa Fé to California with his fruit and other staples,
and is a godsend in a thirsty land.   And while changing his modern fruit into modern dollars, he still
trudges three hundred miles to Moqui to pay turquoise or shell currency for mantas.   He sometimes
carries the paradox even further, and acquires a quiet
revenue by manufacturing fetiches to sell the Bureau
of Ethnology and other seekers after truth.

The most important ethnologic effect of the coming of Spain, was to make the Pueblo from a sedentary to a *fixed* Indian.   Instead of continuing to play
chess with his cities across a three-hundred-mile
board, he now was limited.   To each of his communities was given a generous grant of land, and
upon that grant he must stay.   Thenceforth there
were no town-migrations, and the living pueblos are
essentially where they were when Plymouth Rock
came into history.   These grants have since been
confirmed by our Government ; and the Pueblo is an
Indian who lives not upon a reservation but upon a
United States patent.   The total amount of land
owned by the Pueblos is 893,130 acres.   Zuñi has
215,040 ; Isleta, 110,080 ; Acoma, 95,791 ; and the
smaller towns in proportion.   Of course the vast
majority of this land is fit for nothing but grazing ;
the average tillage of the Pueblo, according to the
guesses of the Census Bureau, is four and a half acres

per capita. Furthermore, the Pueblos are citizens of
the United States, a political fact which seems to
have escaped the notice of the Interior Department
as completely as has the fact that they are members
of a Christian church. Their autonomy and their full
rights of citizenship have been established in the
highest tribunals of the land; and yet we continue to
" educate" them by force, and to send missionaries to
them!

Permanency thus secured by the grant policy, a
further Spanish measure for the benefit of the Pueblos was centralization, which was effected, as usual,
by suasion and not by force. At the Conquest there
were seventy-six inhabited pueblos. One of the first
steps of the missionaries was to induce the Indians to
concentrate in their chief towns, for greater safety
from their savage neighbors; and the result has been
the twenty-four present pueblos. The ethnologic effect upon the Indian of this twofold change has been
very striking. It made him more secure; therefore
more adaptive. It enabled his wholesale conversion
to Christianity—his is the only race of Indian church-
members in our history—and his general material advance. With greater fixity of abode he has still further increased the distance between himself and the
nomad. His perceptions have grown less acute than
those of the hunted hunter—though still far ahead of
the Caucasian—but he has reflected more, acquired
more, and preserved more. His traditions have accumulated to a huge mass; his laws are well formulated; his internal religion has become bewilderingly
complex. It is fortunate for archæology that the
Spaniard was his brother's keeper. Had the Pueblo

enjoyed sixteenth - century acquaintance with the
Saxon, we should be limited now to unearthing and
articulating his bones.

The Pueblo has, more than any of our other aborigines, a home-life; but this also is a gift of Spain.
At the Conquest he maintained rigid separation of
the sexes.   Connecticut laws were a mild blue to his
indigo.   The men and youth slept, ate, and lived in
the *estufa;* the women and children were relegated
to the small rooms of the huge honey-combed pyra-
mid of the terraced house.   The Spanish changed all
this; and to-day the Pueblo lives at home and takes
as much joy thereof as we of ours.

Popular institutions were before us, even in our
own land.   Before history was, this peculiar people
had solved the problem in its own peculiar way; and
there were hundreds of American "republics" ahead
of Columbus.   Every Pueblo town was an autonomic
commonwealth, and is so still—oases of approximate
civilization in a continental desert of savagery.   The
Pueblo social organization is essentially democratic.
It is too complex to enter here—a volume could
scarce contain it—but it may be briefly defined as a
military democracy, guided by a democratic theocra-
cy.   "Church and State" in the Indian sense are distinct yet inseparable.   Moses the captain, and Aaron
the high-priest, are here Siamese twins—two, yet in-
divisible.   The commander-in-chief of the army has
no hampering by Congress; but he would not think
of moving without his chaplain.   There is no absolute head, and a bewildering amount of body in this
remarkable economy.   The actual Captain of War,
Kah-báy-deh, is the highest single man, and within

limits is supreme; but neither is he independent of the Shamans of War, the Cacique, and other officials. He, like all the most potent authorities, holds a life-office; but there is also a figure-head War-Captain who is elected annually, as is the civil governor, both being Spanish innovations dating from 1620. It is a curious fact that the first republican institution in the United States, an annual election of governors, should have come directly from the Spanish Crown. There is no such thing as chiefship. With the Pueblo (as with all aborigines) heredity counts for nothing. All dignities are reached by election, or—in their inner cults—by selection. There is constant watchfulness against any dynastic tendency. More than anywhere in civilization, the official is server of the people, and he is never recreant to his trust.

There is a congress, called the Junta of Principales, which is the civil law-making body, but cannot touch matters of religion. The Governor is chairman of its sessions. The Cacique selects its members; but it retains or impeaches, and ousts them at will. Around these factors of government, and including some of them, cluster the four great orders—the Mothers (three Caciques and the Shamans of War), the Warriors, the Hunters, and the Medicine-men—and again intertangled with these, but below them, a dizzy array of still potent groups which figure in the political economy.

The laws of the pueblo are simple but admirable, and are thoroughly enforced. Crime is practically unknown; and for occasional minor lapses the offender is induced to jail by a handcuff more civilized than our own, since it fits about the neck, and the culprit can neither be tortured by it, nor reach nor pull back upon his captors. The gentleness of officials and laymen is always notable. A resister is never clubbed or choked into acquiescence, but is overpowered without a scratch. A drunken vagabond once shot a woman in Isleta and fled. A posse with rifles pursued and soon overtook him.

A TIGUA GIRL.

He entrenched himself and was ready to shoot the first who should come near. Instead of silencing

him with a bullet, as there was perfect justice in
doing, the Alguazil ordered him dislodged with
stones. A deft throw stunned him, and he was
captured with one unimportant bruise. This is a
typical case.

The social corner-stone is not the family, but the
clan. Husband and wife must belong to different
gentes, and the children follow her clan. In other
words, descent is from the mother, and not from the
father. The Pueblo had invented Woman's Rights before *any* Caucasian acquired that social insomnia, and
it remains one of his fundaments. He has never used
his wife as a pack-beast. He is not henpecked, but
just; and even finds no shame in "toting" the baby
upon his back all day when he has no more essential
duty. The spheres of the sexes are clearly defined,
but manfully. The woman is complete owner of the
house and all it contains save his personal trinkets;
and she has no other work to do than housework, at
which she is no sloven. Should her husband ill-treat
her, she could permanently evict him from home, and
would be upheld in so doing. The man tills the
fields, and they are his; but after the crops are
housed she has an equal voice in their disposition.
The live-stock is, of course, his; but he will seldom
sell an animal without consulting his wife. The family relations are very beautiful. Here are children
never spoiled, never disobedient, almost never quarrelsome; parents never neglectful and never harsh;
and none who fail of respect to seniority—even as
between boy and elder boy. Conjugal fidelity is as
general as with us—the Pueblo was a prehistoric
monogam, and punished unfaithfulness with death—

and it is doubtful if any American community can
show a less percentage of loose women.

The theology of the Pueblos is as democratic as
their sociology, and as complex. Duality is an integral part of their elder religion as of their government. We have seen the idea even in architecture,
where the houses once had gender. The very creation is based on sex. There is no one God*—the
Sun-Father and the Moon-Mother were the equal
First Causes. Their sons, the Hero Twins, seem to
come next in importance; and behind the aboriginal
Castor and Pollux marches a countless host of minor
deities—spirits of every attribute and forms of every
shape. The compass has six cardinal points—East,
North, West, South, Up, and Down-and-around, in
that sacred and inviolable order—and each is the
Olympus of a community of The Trues. The forces
of the universe, the processes of nature, the very
animals of use or danger—all are deified. And with
this astoundingly complicated mythology of infinite
detail the Pueblo has also his Christian *Tata Dios*.
He is as sincere Catholic as pagan, though the pagan
is naturally innermost; and woe to them that would
profane his church, for which he will give his life.
He is baptized, confessed, married, and buried in that
church; and for all has another set of secret ceremonies of his own. It is another phase of this racial
contradiction, this human hyphen between the present and the utmost past, who lights his pleasure
cigarette with an Ohio match, and his medicine
smoke from the prehistoric fire-drill; who hunts with

* Nor did any Indian in North America ever have original belief in one
'Great Spirit."

the Winchester and executes with the obsidian-tipped
arrow ; who goes to mass in the great adobe church
his patient fathers builded for the new faith, and
thence to his feathered prayer-sticks in a mountain
cave.   He has his Christian priest, and then an army
of semi-religious officials to meet every minutest
exigency of life—even to the propagation of the race !
Life is one endless religious ceremony.   The Indian
(and I mean here *any* Indian) does nothing "for
fun."   His hunts, his dances, his races, his very
smoking, have all a deep inner significance.   And
yet he seems secondarily to enjoy it all.   He is an
admirable athlete, and his sports are thrilling, while
his endurance is marvellous.   In his ceremonial spring
foot-races he runs a three-hundred-and-twenty yard
course at a sprinting gait twenty to thirty times in an
afternoon.   His sedentary games are few but good ;
and one is fully equal to chess.   He is not a gambler
like the Navajo ; and though he sometimes bets, it is
seldom on a game of simple chance.   Nor is he a
politician.   Here in very truth the office seeks the
man.   Not uncommonly a governor has to be thrown
for a few days into the *calaboz* before he will accept the
high office to which he has just been elected.   This
election is by the Junta ; but there is already a growing sentiment toward universal suffrage.   The present Governor of the large pueblo of Isleta belongs to
the radical "Gophers," who favor this change, while
the conservative "Black-Eyes" oppose it.   The two
parties are about equal in numbers.   The office of
Cacique is still more difficult to be forced upon the
appointee.   He is not a ruler, as popularly imagined,
but the tribal penitent, whose life of incessant self-

mortification and hardship is not to be coveted, despite his great influence.

They were never more mistaken who deem the Pueblo dull. He has even a poetic imagination. His folk-lore is not only vastly voluminous, but full of fancy—at times, of striking beauty. It is poetry in body as well as in spirit; for it is told down from father to son in fixed metrical form, though not in rhyme. He is also a deep humorist; and in the proper time and place a very genial one. He is an aboriginal Uncle Remus, full of quaint fables wherein the coyote is the butt of all jokes and is *burlado* by every other animal. He is himself a joker upon occasion, and as an official clown in certain ceremonies is a real genius. Above all, he recognizes the humor of self-containing. We find a joke or a sensation, and forthwith itch to set someone else agape. The Indian finds it more humorous to laugh himself and let the other fellow go bump his head in perplexity as to what it is all about—which is a double philosophy. But when he condescends to be funny he is no failure. His very nicknames are not those of the stupid. He calls the Navajo—who never knows water as a means of grace—"Dried-up-and-cracked-Skin." The Caucasian is Hlah-fáh-deh, "Hair-mouth;" and the Mexican, specifically, Pee-peéd-deh, the "Wet-Head" (in allusion, of course, to baptism). The people of Zuñi are officially known in Tigua as the "Scratchers," and Zuñi as "Scratch-town"—an ill-compliment which is too true of Zuñi as compared with the cleanlier other pueblos. There is even sarcasm sometimes in the nomenclature of animals; and the duck is "Old-Man-Afraid-of-the-Water."

A HOUSE AT SANTO DOMINGO.

Folk-songs are as popular as folk-stories, but never humorous, save in occasional improvisation. The Pueblo is almost always a singer; and bitter indeed must be the night when you will not find, upon every broom-built hillock in the village, knots of young men chanting in unison, with strong, clear voices, their

Háy-nah én-neh háy-nah.

Even "bees" prevail. The corn-husking is done thus with the aid of young men who go from house to house to strip the blue ears, and roll their cigarros in the rustling husks, and sing loudly as they work. The women used to join also for their winter's grinding. Each brought to an appointed house her *metate* and sack of corn. And as the kernels fell to blue meal between the lava slabs, there rose a poetic song of the birth of corn, swelled by the men, who kept time with tap of the hammer as they shaped rawhide soles for their *teguas*.

One of these *metate* songs, literally translated, is as follows:

> How-háy-eh, yow-ow-áh,
> Hay yow yoo-oo,
> Sai lee ee.*
> Is it not beautiful? ⎫
> Is it not, truly! ⎬ Repeat five times.
> On every side They are,
> The Trues, the rain-commanders.
> Do you not hear their drum? †
> Because of that you will see
> This year the vapor floating;
> Because of that you will see

---

* Refrain not understood by the singers here. It is probably borrowed from some other language.　　　　† The thunder.

This year the drizzling rain.
  Is it not beautiful?
  Is it not, truly!
In all the fields the corn upspringing
Like the young pine it comes up ;
Like the green aspen ;
In all the fields the corn upspringing,
Tall like the tail of the thrush ;
Tall like the road-runner's tail,*
In all the fields the corn upspringing !
  Hay ow yow how hay,
  Yay yay yay yay,
  Yow how how how.

With all this gregariousness, the villages even of the same tribal stock are entirely independent and aloof from each other. There are six Pueblo stocks, each with an entirely distinct language of its own, and understanding the others only through the diplomatic Spanish—and yet they are racially one. The Quéres are by far the most numerous, counting over three thousand souls, and with seven towns. Next come the Tiguas and the Moquis, with less than two thousand people each, and four and six towns respectively ; the Tehuas, with about one thousand five hundred in five villages ; the Zuñis, with one town of one thousand five hundred inhabitants ; and Jemez one with a third as many. The towns of the same tribe are not even always adjacent. Isleta and Taos are the southern and northern extremes of present Pueblo range ; and between these chief Tigua towns are eleven villages of the Tehuas and the Quéres.

The characteristic architecture which the Pueblo had evolved before history has been influenced only downward by civilization. His astonishing communal

---

* A small pheasant.

house has altogether disappeared in several villages.
Taos is the most striking example left of the one-

TIGUA GIRLS.

house town ; and its two villages, one on either side
the rippling trout-brook, are, as Coronado found

them, each of a huge, six-story pyramid house. In
Zuñi the five-story pyramidal honey-comb is still potent, though clustered upon by detached blocks.
Acoma, the peerless cliff-built citadel of the Quéres,
is in three blocks of three terraces each. The pyra-
mid, the block, the once still commoner rectangle—
with sheer walls without, and the terraces and doors
facing only the safe plaza—and the invariable defen-
sive site are eloquent witnesses to the dangers of
old, when every first thought must be for safety from
the crowding savage. Convenience, even to water,
was a secondary consideration. Of this, Acoma is
the most striking type. No other town on earth is
so nobly perched. The only foreign hints of it are
the Königstein, in Saxony; and (perhaps) the Gwa-
lior, in the Deccan. And these are not so like it as
are the Moqui towns, which are still far less noble
than Acoma.

Along the Rio Grande, however, the communal
building has largely given way to separate homes of
one or two stories, but larger rooms. Even here the
Pueblo architecture is distinguishable from the Mexican, and in artistic effect superior to it.

With a background so invariably striking that the
stranger to his history might well deem his choice of
sites to have been dominated by the scenery—for he
has chosen always the most picturesque points of a
picturesque land—the Pueblo is personally in accord.
He is the most—almost the only—picturesque figure
in our conventionalized land. Of medium but robust
stature, admirable neck and trunk, never consumptive,
scarcely ever too fat, with magnificent black hair,
which is not coarse and never leaves him unthatched,

he is physically above the average of his new neighbors, and lives to a vast age.   His face is very far
from our idea of an Indian physiognomy, and is a
creditable index to his contents.   His national cos-
tume, when unspoiled by "civilized" perversions, is
an artistic joy.
There is no
name for the
"policy" which
forcibly changes
the Pueblo girl
at school (a citi-
zen, remember)
from her own
modest, artistic,
Oriental dress
to a gingham
horror, not
worth a tenth as
much in money
or taste; and the
sin is scarce
smaller toward
the boys.   The
home dress of
both sexes is far
ahead of ours

A PUEBLO NIMROD.

hygienically and in convenience.   The garb of a
Pueblo woman at home is worth twenty-five dollars
or more ; and her feast-day array several times that.
To this the aboriginal jewelry largely contributes.
Gold has never been used ; but of silver, coral, and
turquoise ornaments, the Pueblos own much over

$100,000 worth. The silver rosaries, bracelets, rings, ear-rings, buttons, etc., are made by their own silver-smiths, who achieve remarkable results with a mud forge, a hammer, a file, a punch, and a little solder, resin, and acid. The turquoise is also worked into beads by their own artisans.

Money, of course, is less commonly accumulated; yet I know Pueblos who have great chests full of gold and silver coin; and the largest business controlled by any woman in New Mexico is that of Doña Marcelina Abeita, of Isleta, an uneducated Indian woman. She keeps, as all her people keep, her ledger in her head, and with never a mistake of overcharge or omission. A Pueblo sometimes takes temporary service as a laborer for the superior race. Quite as often he hires Mexicans to assist in his own work.

These are but hints of the Pueblo. Actual description of him is not for a book but a library. I have meant here merely to graze the angles of his entity, sketchily but truthfully, in the light of present science, whereby he has not yet been popularly viewed; and even that, with chief reference to the qualities of body and mind, heart and pocket, which entitle him to foremost rank as "Lo" who is *not* "Poor."

III

THE CITY IN THE SKY

THE CITY IN THE SKY

THERE is one Acoma.* It is a class by itself. The peer of it is not in the world. I might call it the Quéres Gibraltar ; but Gibraltar is a pregnable place beside it. It is the Quebec of the Southwest ; but Quebec could be stormed in the time an army climbed Acoma unopposed. If as a defensible town there be no standard whereby to measure it, comparison is still more hopeless when we attack its impregnable beauty and picturesqueness. It is the Garden of the Gods multiplied by ten, and with ten equal but other wonders thrown in ; plus a human interest, an archæological value, an atmosphere of romance and mystery. It is a labyrinth of wonders of which no person alive knows all, and of which not six white men have even an adequate conception, though hundreds have seen it in part. The longest visit never wears out its glamour : one feels as in a strange, sweet, unearthly dream—as among scenes and beings more than human, whose very rocks are genii, and whose people swart conjurors. It is spendthrift of beauty. There are half a hundred cattle and sheep corrals, whose surroundings would be the fortune of as many summer-resorts in the East ; and scores of untrodden cliff-sentinelled gorges far grander yet.

* Pronounced Ah-co-mah ; accent on first syllable.

If there is any sight in the world which will cling to one, undimmed by later impressions, it is the first view of Acoma and its valley from the *mesa* * as one comes in from the west. After the long, slow slope among the sprawling cedars, one stands suddenly upon a smooth divide, looking out upon such a scene as is nowhere else. A few rods ahead, the *mesa* breaks down in a swift cliff of six hundred feet to a valley that seems surely enchanted. A grassy trough, five miles wide and ten in visible length, smooth with that ineffable hazy smoothness which is only of the Southwest, crowded upon by noble precipices, patched with exquisite hues of rocks and clays and growing crops—it is such a vista as would be impossible outside the arid lands. And in its midst lies a shadowy world of crags so unearthly beautiful, so weird, so unique, that it is hard for the onlooker to believe himself in America, or upon this dull planet at all. As the evening shadows play hide-and-seek among those towering sandstones it is as if an army of Titans marched across the enchanted plain. To the left beetles the vast cliff of Kat-zí-mo, or the Mesa Encantada, the noblest single rock in America ; to the right, the tall portals of two fine cañons, themselves treasure-houses of wonders ; between, the chaos of the buttes that flank the superb *mesa* of Acoma. That is one rock —a dizzy air-island above the plain—three hundred and fifty-seven feet high, seventy acres in area upon its irregular but practically level top—a stone table upheld by ineffable precipices which are not merely perpendicular but in great part actually overhanging. The contour of those cliffs is an endless enchantment.

* Table-land with cliff sides.

THE EAST CLIFF OF ACOMA : MESA ENCANTADA IN THE DISTANCE.

They are broken by scores of marvellous bays, scores
of terrific columns and pinnacles, crags and towers.
There are dozens of " natural bridges," from one of a
fathom's span to one so sublime, so crushing in its
savage and enormous grandeur, that the heart fairly
stops beating at first sight of it. There are strange
standing rocks and balanced rocks, vast *potreros* and
fairy minarets, wonderlands of recesses, and mysterious caves. It is the noblest specimen of fantastic
erosion on the continent. Everywhere there is in-
sistent suggestion of Assyrian sculpture in its rocks.
One might fancy it a giant Babylon, water-worn to
dimness. The peculiar cleavage of its beautiful sandstone has hemmed it with strange top-heavy statues
that guard grim chasms. The invariable approach of
visitors is to the tamest side of the *mesa ;* and *that*
surpasses what one shall find elsewhere. But to out-
do one's wildest dreams of the picturesque, one should
explore the whole circumference of the mesa, which
not a half a dozen Americans have ever done. No
one has ever exhausted Acoma; those who know it
best are forever stumbling upon new glories.

Upon the bare table-top of this strange stone island
of the desert, seven thousand feet above the level of
the sea, stands a town of matchless interest—the home
of half a thousand quaint lives, and of half a thousand
years' romance. How old is that mysterious sky city
no man may know. In the far gray past Acoma
stood atop the Mesa Encantada, three miles north ;
but a mighty throe of nature toppled down the vast
ladder-rock which gave sole adit to that dizzy perch—
twice as high as the now Acoma. The people were
left homeless in the plain, where they were tending

their crops; and three doomed women, left at home,
were shut aloft to perish upon the accursed cliff. But
when the Spanish world-finders saw this magic valley
the present Acoma was already an ancient city, from
whose eternal battlements the painted natives looked
down upon the mailed invaders by as many hundreds
of feet as centuries have since then faded. There
stand, so far aloft, the quaint homes of six hundred
people—three giant blocks of stone and adobe, running east and west near a thousand feet, and skyward
forty—and their huge church. When one has climbed
the *mesa* to the town and grasped its proportions,
wonder grows to amaze. No other town in the world
is reached only by such vertiginous trails, or rather
by such ladders of the rock; and yet up these awful
paths the patient Quéres have brought upon their
backs every timber, every stone, every bit of adobe
mud to build that strange city and its marvellous
church. There are timbers fourteen inches square
and forty feet long, brought by human muscle alone
from the mountains twenty miles away. The church
walls are sixty feet high and ten feet through; and
the building covers more ground than any modern
cathedral in the United States. The graveyard in
front, nearly two hundred feet square, took forty years
in the building; for first the gentle toilers had to frame
a giant box with stone walls, a box forty feet deep at
the outer edge, and then to fill it backful by backful
with earth from the far plain. In the weird stone
"ladders" by which the top of the cliff is reached,
the patient moccasined feet of forgotten centuries
have sunk their imprint six inches deep in the rock.
Antiquity and mystery haunt every nook. The very

air is hazy with romance. How have they lived and loved and suffered here in their skyward home, these quiet Hano Oshatch—the Children of the Sun.

Acoma is thirteen miles south of the Atlantic & Pacific Railroad, in the western half of New Mexico. The best stations from which to reach it are Laguna (its daughter pueblo) and McCarty's, from either of which places an Indian may be procured to transport the visitor by farm-wagon.

Acoma figures in our very first knowledge of the Southwest; and the earliest European eyes that ever saw it marvelled as we marvel yet. In spite of the closet historians, Cabeza de Vaca never saw New Mexico. The heroic Franciscan, Fray Marcos of Nizza, in 1539, was the first civilized man who ever looked upon that strangest landmark of our antiquity, a Pueblo town. But he never got beyond the pueblos of Zuñi—the famed " Seven Cities of Cibola "— though he heard of Acoma. In 1540 the most remarkable of all explorers of North America, Francisco Vasquez Coronado, saw Zuñi, and a little later came to the more wondrous town of which the Zuñis had told him—Há-cu-que, Ah-co, Acoma. Of its salient wonders he has left us a very accurate description. We may well imagine that the awestruck savages were no more astounded at their first sight of fair-faced strangers than were the latter at that thrice-wondrous town. There were grizzled veterans there who had been with the Great Captain, Cortez, in his conquest of the southern wonderland; but they had never found anything like this. The adobe city of Motecuzoma, in the bloody lake of Tezcuco—it was bigger, but what was it to this sky-built citadel?

That with its strong walls and narrow dykes was ill enough to storm, and worse to retreat from ; but what would be a Noche Triste among these grim cliffs ? Fortunately, there was no need to learn. The Acomas received the wondrous strangers kindly, taking them for gods; and Coronado and his heroic little band pressed on unmolested to the Rio Grande and to their unprecedented march of exploration in chase of the gilded myth of the Quivíra.

It was near half a century after Coronado's gallant but ill-starred exploits before the adventurous Spaniards were again tempted to the discouraging deserts of our Southwest. Truly there was little enough to tempt them! Utterly disappointed in the golden hopes which had led them to such rovings as no other nation paralleled anywhere, and, finding almost as little of other attractions as of gold, they long devoted themselves to the more grateful countries to our south. It was not until that pre-eminent figure among the colonizers of North America, the unspoiled millionaire Juan de Oñate, came with his five-hundred-thousand-dollar expedition, that permanent work began to be done in New Mexico ; though before him, and after Coronado, Chamuscado, Espejo, and de Sosa had made notable successive explorations here. In 1581 Espejo visited Acoma, and there saw the astounding snake-dance which now survives alone in remote Moqui—a dance wherein the half-naked performers bear living, mortal rattlesnakes in their hands and mouths. Espejo also was well treated in Acoma, and gave us a good description of its wonders, though his guess at the population was as wild as his guesses at the other pueblos. He was the one

glaring exception to the painstaking accuracy of the
Spanish explorers in their chronicles of wonders seen.

The first real foothold of Europeans in Acoma was
achieved in 1598, when the Acomas voluntarily sub-
mitted themselves to the authority of Oñate and became vassals of the Spanish crown, swearing to the
Act of Obedience, whose purport was fully explained
to them. But the submission was not in good faith.
The Indians had no idea of real surrender; but these
stranger Men-of-Power might not be openly opposed,
and it was best to move by treachery. The war captains had already laid their plans to entrap and slay
Oñate, believing that his death would materially
weaken the Spaniards. But Oñate's lucky star led
him out of the unsuspected danger; and with his wee
army he proceeded on that grim desert march to
Moqui.

Scarcely had he gone when his lieutenant, Juan de
Zaldivar, arrived with a dozen men from a vast journey. The Acomas enticed them up into the town,
fell upon them by daylight, and bungled them to
death with clubs and flint knives. Five bleeding
heroes leaped down the ghastly cliff—a leap unparalleled. Wonderful to tell, only one was killed by that
incredible fall; the remaining four lived, and finally
escaped.

In the following month—as soon as the weak Spanish resources could be marshalled—Oñate sent a little band to punish treacherous Acoma. Never did
soldiers march to a forlorner hope; and never in all
history was there a greater feat of arms than the
storming of that impregnable rock by Vicente de
Zaldivar with seventy men—of whom less than three-

score were engaged in the assault—on the bloody
22d, 23d, and 24th of January, 1599.   The forcing of
that awful cliff, the three days' death-struggle hand-
to-hand, the storming of that fortress-town room by
savage room—time records nothing more desper-
ately brilliant.   These smooth, gray rocks, whereon
I dream to-day, were slippery-red then with the life-
blood of five hundred heroes—for here Greek met
Greek—and ghastly rivulets ran down the hollows
and trickled over the cliff to the thirsty valley.   This
drowsy air was split with the war-cry of Santiago
and the shrill enemy-yell of the Hero Brothers; and
where yon naked babes sport dimpled in a dim-
pling pool, stark warriors wallowed in a grimmer bath,
and gasped from dying lips undying hate.   Over yon
dizzy brink I toss unanswering pebbles to the deep
plain, where maddened savages sprang forth to death
in spatters.   And where yon statuesque maiden
walks placidly, a great gay *tinaja* of water perched
upon her shapely head, a gray, tattered, bleeding
Spaniard received the surrender of the scant remnant
of crushed Acoma.   In the precious epic left by Villa-
gran, the soldier poet, who was *pars magna* of those
bitter days, we have still a long and graphic description of a heroism which history could ill afford
to lose.

Thirty years later there was another capture of
Acoma, as remarkable and as heroic as Zaldivar's
marvellous assault, but with other weapons.   In that
year of 1629 came the apostle of the Acomas, brave,
gentle Fray Juan Ramirez, walking his perilous way
alone from distant Santa Fé.   His new parishioners
received him with a storm of arrows.   There is a cur-

rent legend that they threw him off the cliff, and that
his priestly robes upheld him miraculously and saved
his life ; but this is a myth without foundation of fact.
It probably sprang, partly, from confusion with the
marvellous and real escape of Oñate's four men who
leaped over the cliff and lived, and partly from a mis-
understanding of the Indian folk - lore. The un-
daunted Franciscan faced the wrath of the savages,
and finally won their hearts. For a score of years
he lived alone among them, taught them to read and
write, and led them to Christianity. The first church
in Acoma, built two centuries and a half ago, was one
of the monuments of this as noble and successful
missionary as ever lived.

And then came the awful month of Santana, 1680,
when the Pueblo thunderbolt burst from a clear sky
upon the doomed Spaniards. Nowhere else in the
history of the United States, save at the Little Big-
horn, was there such a massacre of Caucasians by
Indians as on that red 10th of August. More than a
score of devoted missionaries, more than four hundred heroic Spanish colonists, were butchered then,
in a blow that fell across all New Mexico at once ;
and the pitiful remnant of the invader was driven
from the land. In Acoma was then the good Franciscan, Fray Lucas Maldonado. How his treacherous flock fell upon the lone martyr ; if they thrust
him off the wild precipice that girt his parish (as
their own legend says), or beat out life from the quiv-
ering clay with clubs and stones, or spilt it from
gashes with the cruel flint knife, we may never know.
All that is left to us is the knowledge that he was
slaughtered here, and here fills an unknown grave ;

and that the dearly built temple of the white God was razed to the earth.   With it went the thumbed church-books, that would have been so precious to history and to romance to-day.

When Diego de Vargas, the re-conqueror, took back New Mexico in 1692, Acoma surrendered at once to his formidable force of two hundred men.   In 1696 the high-perched pueblo again rebelled.   Vargas marched against it, but could not storm the deadly rock ; and the rebellion was never punished. The Acomas, however, seeing all the other pueblos submitting to the humane invader, gradually relented from their defiance and fell into line.   The mission was re-established, and the church rebuilt, about the year 1700.   Since then the quaint town has dwelt in peace.   In 1728 was the last attempt at a Pueblo up-rising, but in that Acoma was not concerned ; and the Franciscan Fathers labored undisturbed in their lonely field.   The last Franciscan in New Mexico, Fray Mariano de Jesus Lopez, was priest of Acoma more than a generation ago.   He it was who settled the strange quarrel between Acoma and Laguna over the possession of the oil painting of San José, pre-sented by Charles II. of Spain to the Indians three-quarters of a century before—a remarkable case, which figures interestingly in the reports of the Su-preme Court of New Mexico.   The good old fraile met death by the accidental discharge of a venerable pistol.

Laguna, by the way—itself a very interesting spot, directly upon the A. & P. R. R., where its strange architecture is the wonder of thousands of travellers —is the newest of all the pueblos.   It was founded

July 4, 1699, by refugees from Acoma (which contrib-
uted a large majority), Zia, and Cochití.   Later it
received recruits also from Zuñi.

The people of Acoma are quaint as their remarkable
city.   In their very simplicity breathes an atmosphere
of the mysterious.   Tangibly they are plain, indus-
trious farmers, strongly Egyptian in their methods,
despite the steel plough and the Studebacker wagon
of recent adoption.   Their lands are 95,791 acres,
confirmed by United States patent.   Of this area the
great majority is available only for grazing ; but the
valley wherein the mesa stands, the well-watered valley of the San José, twelve miles northwest, wherein
is their summer pueblo of Acomita, and some minor
areas, are threaded with irrigating ditches, and rustle
with corn and wheat, chile, beans, and wee peach
orchards and melon patches.   Their crops are adequate.   They have enough to eat, enough to sell for
luxuries.   The dark store-rooms in their curious
houses are never empty ; and in the living-rooms
hang queer *tasajos* (twists) of dried muskmelon for
dwarf pies, bags of dried peaches for the same end,
jerked mutton from their own flocks, jerked venison
from the communal hunt, parched chile, and other
staples.   In a corner is always the row of sloping
lava slabs, neatly boxed about, whereon the blue corn
is rubbed to meal with a smaller slab.   Along the
walls hang buckskins and Moqui - woven mantas,*
cougar-skin bow-cases beside the Winchester, coral
necklaces and solid silver necklaces, the work of their
own clever smiths, and many other aboriginal treasures.   The cleanly and comfortable wool mattresses

* Dress of Pueblo women.

are rolled and laid on benches with handsome and often costly Navajo blankets, for a daytime sofa. By night they are unrolled upon rugs or canvases on the floor. In one corner is the wee but effective adobe fireplace, with chimney generally of unbottomed earthen jars, and in another a row of handsome *tinajas*, painted in strange patterns, full of fresh water.

Outside, the house is even more picturesque. Each building is solid for several hundred feet, but cut by cross-walls into separate little homes which never have interior communication with each other. The block is three stories high, with a sheer wall behind but terraced in front, so that it looks like a flight of three gigantic steps. Save in a very few cases of recent innovation, there are no doors to the lower floor; and the only entrance to a house is by ladder to the roof of the first story, well back upon which the second story opens. The only entrance to the first story is through a tiny trap-door in the floor of the second and down a ladder. The third story and the utmost roof are reached by queer little steps on the division walls. The doors are nearly all very tiny, and the windows, save of a few spoiled houses, are merely big sheets of translucent gypsum, set solidly into the opening.

The costumes of the people are strikingly picturesque, and even handsome. That of the women in particular is Oriental, characteristic, and modest. Not only that, but it is costly. These quiet folks, whose facial appearance is generally comely, are far from naked savages.

The main mesa of Acoma is an indented oval; but at the south it is half yoked by an impassable hyphen

A GLIMPSE OF ACOMA.

of crags to a similar and equally noble mesa.   So the
whole rock, at a bird's-eye view, strikingly resembles,
in shape, a pair of bowed spectacles.   There are no
dwellings on the southern mesa ; but thither leads—
down the side of the crag-hyphen and up again
—a trail, deep worn in the rock, to the great reservoir, chief of the many hollows which serve Acoma
for water-works.   This reservoir—a picturesquely
beautiful cavity in the solid rock—should be seen at
sunrise, when the strange lights and shadows, the
clear image of its bluff walls in the mirror of a lakelet
make it a vision never to be forgotten.   On the main
mesa are a great many somewhat similar tanks, large
and small ; the natural capacity of the larger ones increased by damming.   Those nearest the houses are
used as the town washtubs for clothing and children
—for the Acomas are cleanly—and the farther ones
for drinking-water, of which the great tank on the
south mesa, however, furnishes the main supply.   In
the high, dry air of this altitude, these natural stone
reservoirs keep the rain-water cool and fresh the
whole year around; and the supply almost never fails.
When it does, there are fine springs in the plain
whereupon to draw.   Every drop of water used in
the houses is brought by the women in three to five
gallon *tinajas* upon their heads—an exercise which
may be largely responsible for the superb necks and
chests and the confident poise of head notable among
all Pueblo women.   There is no more picturesque
sight than the long file of these comely maids and
matrons marching homeward in the sunset glow with
their careless head-burdens.

Across the far, smooth valley the curling gramma

FAUSTINO, WAR CAPTAIN OF ACOMA.

AN ACOMA MAIDEN.

JUANICO, A PRINCIPAL.

ACOMA TYPES.

is dotted with broad herds of horses, cattle, burros;
and back in the surrounding wilderness of table-lands
are great flocks of sheep.   Nightly, as the sun falls
back upon the huge black pillow of the Mesa Prieta,
the hundreds of horses and burros are driven to the
mesa's top by a new trail which has been builded
with infinite toil since peace came.   By the old trails
—which sufficed the town for unknown centuries—
not even a goat could mount the giant rock.

Such, to the casual sight, are the folk of Acoma,
and such their surroundings ; but, as one looks, there
grows consciousness of the mystery within.   Here
and there are windowless rooms, reached only by a
trapdoor in the roof and by a tall, rude ladder topped
with mystic symbols.   No stranger may enter there ;
but white-headed *principales* climb in and out, and
strange muffled songs float off over the housetops far
into the night, with now and then the dull beat of the
tombé ; and now and then is the watcher aware of
an invisible spiral of smoke curling above the dark
hatchway—from the sacred fire that never died nor
ever shall.   When Pa-yát-ya-ma, the Sun Father,
shows his ruddy face above the eastern mesas, and
again when he sinks into the dark ridges of the west,
there are stirless human statues upon the housetops
that show for more than careless lookouts.   In the
houses are mysterious symbols which the stranger
dare not touch.   In wild cave shrines above and below the cliffs are thousands of unknowable sticks
tufted with downy feathers, miniature bows and arrows like those of Mau-sa-we and O-ya-we, and wee
imitations of the magic hoop.   Quaint, tiny parcels of
the sacred corn-meal, wrapped and tied with the pre-

cious husk, are stowed everywhere in crannies of the
infinite rocks. Everywhere are these hints of solemn
mysteries, into which the visitor shall do well not to
pry. In a dizzy eyrie of the southern mesa, safe
enough from the inquisitive, is perched a perfect
cliff-house—startling link back to antiquity. Few
strangers have ever seen it; few ever will, for the
climbing is a neck's worth; but there it is, gray, impassive relict of the Forgotten. There are strange,
symbolic foot-races and stranger dances, the least of
which the world may see on the feast of San Esteban,
the patron saint of Acoma, September 2d, and on
other holy days; but upon the chief ones no stranger
has ever looked. They are more secret than the
Inquisition.

Beside the sun-seared graveyard, where the dead
of centuries sleep unmindful that their crowded bones
are jostled by each new-comer unto rest, is a miniature mountain of breakage. If you watch when the
still form, swathed in its costliest blanket, has been
lowered into its narrow bed; when upon the earthen
coverlet has been broken the symbolic jar of water;
when from the tottering belfry has pealed the last
silver clang of the high bell with its legend, " San
Pedro, año 1710 ; " when the wailing mourners have
filed away to the desolate house where the Shamans
are blinding the eyes of the ghosts, that they may
not find the trail of the evanished soul on its four-
days' journey to Shi-p'a-pú—then you shall see borne
forth jars and hand-mills and weapons and ornaments
and clothing, to be broken and rent upon the killing-
place, that they may go on with their departed owner.
When old men meet and part you may see that each

takes the other's hand to his mouth and breathes from it; and that when they smoke they blow the first six puffs to different directions. Every man wears a little pouch which money will not unlock. Each knows words which he may not utter aloud in any finite presence. Each has goings out and comings in which none must spy upon.

And so at every turn there are hints and flashes of the unknown and the unknowable, the pettiest of which you shall try in vain to fathom. Their marvellous mythology, their infinitely complicated social, religious, and political economies, their exhaustless and beautiful fore-lore—of all you shall everywhere find clues, but nowhere knowledge. And as the rumbling farm-wagon jolts you back from your enchanted dream to the prosy wide-awake of civilization, you shall go to be forever haunted by that unearthly cliff, that weird city, and their unguessed dwellers.

IV

THE PENITENT BROTHERS

THE PENITENT BROTHERS

" UNTIL recent times the practice of self-flagella-
tion—as a religious custom—continued to
manifest itself intermittently in the south of France,
and also in Italy and Spain ; and so late as 1820 a
procession of flagellants took place at Lisbon." So
the Encyclopædia Britannica winds up what is intended to be a complete outline of the history of self-
whipping as a means of grace.

Aye, verily ! And so late as 1891 a procession of
flagellants took place within the limits of the United
States. A procession in which voters of this Republic shredded their naked backs with savage
whips, staggered beneath huge crosses, and hugged
the maddening needles of the cactus ; a procession
which culminated in the flesh-and-blood crucifixion of
an unworthy representative of the Redeemer. Nor
was this an isolated horror. Every Good Friday, for
many generations, it has been a staple custom to
hold these barbarous rites in parts of New Mexico.

It is surprising that none of the encyclopædias give
a hint of the existence of the Order of Penitents in
the United States. Nor has any book * contained
anything like the truth about this astounding fact.
This ignoring of the subject is the more remarkable

* Except a juvenile of my own, which has a short sketch.

because the institution is no new thing ; and hundreds of Saxon-Americans have witnessed it.

The idea of the whip as a means of grace is one of the oldest in the history of nations. Herodotus tells us that the ancient Egyptians flogged themselves in honor of Isis. The boys of Sparta were whipped before the altar of Artemis Orthia. In the Roman Lupercalia the devout citizens esteemed it a felicity to be struck by the leathern thongs of the Luperci. And by the beginning of the fifth century the Christian church came to recognize the virtues of the lash for offending monks—a remedy to whose efficacy several provincial councils testified. About the end of the eleventh century, Cardinal Peter Damian preached and practised self-whipping as a penance, and inspired a considerable following. About 1210, St. Anthony of Padua founded the first fraternity for regular and public self-practice with the rod as a religious cere-mony. Half a century later the struggling order took a sudden lease of vigorous life in Italy, by the efforts of a Perugian monk named Rainer. Rich and poor walked with leathern whips through the streets of Perugia, whipping themselves until " they drew blood from their tortured bodies amid sighs and tears, sing-ing at the same time penitential psalms and entreating the compassions of the Deity." Penitent pilgrims soon carried the strange infection throughout Italy, Bavaria, Bohemia, Austria, Hungary, and Poland. For a long time their cuticular devotions evoked vast admiration ; but presently Church and State alike for-bade their exhibitions. The eruption broke out again in Hungary after the great plague in the fourteenth century, and spread to Germany. The attempt of 120

Flagellants to convert England to their practices, signally failed. Then the Catholic Church aroused itself in earnest. Pope Clement VI. fulminated a bull against the order in 1349; and under Gregory XI. the Inquisition made it literally so hot for the fanatics that they disappeared. In 1414, Conrad Schmidt and his foremost followers were executed for trying to revive the custom in Thuringia. A mitigated phase of the practice prevailed in France in the sixteenth century; but the fraternities of flagellants seldom whipped in public. It is even of record that Henry III. of France established a whipping brotherhood in Paris and personally participated in its processions— all for political effect. His successor suppressed the fraternities in France; but the spirit of fanaticism has never been entirely dead, and sporadic instances of the custom have been cropping out here and there ever since.

The order of Los Hermanos Penitentes (the Penitent Brothers) was founded in Spain some 300 years ago. It had nothing of the scourge in its original plan. Its members met for religious study and conversation, and were men of good morals and good sense "according to their lights." The seeds of the order were brought to Mexico, and later to what is now New Mexico, by the Franciscan friars with the Spanish *Conquistadores*. The first public penance in New Mexico (as it then was) was by Juan de Oñate and his men, in 1594. By slow degrees the once godly order shrank and grew deformed among the brave but isolated and ingrown people of that lonely land; until the monstrosity of the present fanaticism had devolved.

6

The order was unquestionably of Franciscan origin. In Spanish letters-patent, of as late date as 1793, we find it referred to as "*La Cofradia del tercer orden de Franciscanos*"—the Brotherhood of the Third Order of Franciscans.

It is interesting to note that a tribal penance, vicariously done, has been a custom among the Pueblo Indians from time immemorial, and is still observed. Twice every year, in each of the nineteen now-inhabited pueblos, a penitential fast of four days is kept by allotted parties. In Isleta six men and six women are selected to expiate thus the sins of the whole pueblo; and in some pueblos the whole adult population fasts. Where a small number bear the sins of all, they are shut up in the *estufa* (sacred council-chamber) with a *tinaja* of water before each; but they must not drink. Every morning, a delegation comes to wash their feet. This fast continues four days. It is the only form of penance known to exist among them now, aside from what is imposed by the church.

When the Spanish *conquistadores* first entered New Mexico they found traces of a similar custom, of then great antiquity. All the tribes had their tribal professional penitents. The word *cacique*, so widely misused, means nothing else. The Tanos Indians, whose pueblos then occupied the country about Galisteo—Sante Fé's present site being also included in their territory—were called by a name based on the method of their penance. This name in the Quéres tongue was *Poo-ya-tye*, from *poo-ya*, a thorn. They were the tribe whose *caciques* did penance by pricking themselves with the thorns of the cactus.

Just *how* this pricking was done, is not known. Whether it was by lying on beds of thorns, and lashing prickly burdens to the body, as the Mexican Penitentes do now, or whether merely by jabbing the individual thorn through the cuticle, is still a mystery. Bandelier has thus far discovered nothing which will throw more explicit light on this subject, as the Tanos are now extinct, save at the Tehua pueblo of Moqui.

In old Mexico there is nothing to be compared with the Penitentes. The reign of the *Fariseos*, and the Holy Week representation of the Crucifixion and Resurrection, by life-like automatons, belong in a widely different category.

However the curious devolution was accomplished, it is certain that for over a century there has been in New Mexico an order of Penitentes whose credo was founded upon the whip and the cross as instruments of penance. Up to within a decade the order in this Territory numbered some thousands, with fraternities in towns of every county. Their strongholds were in Taos, Mora and Rio Arriba counties, where ten years ago they numbered respectively 500, 300 and 1,000 members, approximately. Los Griegos, a hamlet just below Albuquerque, was another hot-bed of them, and many dwelt in the fastnesses of the Sandia Mountains east of Albuquerque. In 1867 there were 900 within a radius of ten miles from Taos. Each town had its independent fraternity, ruled by an *Hermano Mayor* (chief brother) who was elected annually by his fellows. He had no superior, and was not even obliged to hold counsel with the neighboring *hermanos mayores*. In scores of lonely

cañons throughout the Territory, the traveler may
see to this day the deserted, low, stone houses with
huge crosses leaning in slow decay against their sides
—tokens of the bloody rites which the surrounding
hills once witnessed.   The order was too strong in
earlier days to be excommunicated at one fell swoop;
and the Catholic Church —to which all the Penitentes
claim allegiance—went at the work with prudent de-
liberation, lopping off a head here and a head there
in a quiet way, which carried its full lesson without
provoking rebellion.   The policy has been a successful one and has been unflinchingly maintained.
Town after town has dropped its Holy Week cele-
brations, fraternity after fraternity has melted away
to nothingness.   In the year 1888 but three towns in
the Territory had Penitente processions; and but one
—San Mateo, in the western end of Valencia County
—enjoyed a crucifixion.

Lent is the sole season of Penitente activity.   The
rest of the year their religion is allowed to lapse in
desuetude more or less innocuous, and the brethren
placidly follow their various vocations as laborers,
cowboys, or shepherds.   With the beginning of the
sacred forty days, however, they enter upon the convenient task of achieving their piety for the year.
Every Friday night in Lent the belated wayfarer
among the interior ranges is liable to be startled by
the hideous too-ootle-te-too of an unearthly whistle
which wails over and over its refrain.

As the midnight wind sweeps that weird strain
down the lonely cañon, it seems the wail of a lost
spirit.   I have known men of tried bravery to flee
from that sound when they heard it for the first time.

A simple air on a fife made of the *cariso* seems a mild matter to read of; but its wild shriek, which can be heard for miles, carries an indescribable terror with it. " The oldest timer " crosses himself and looks askance when that sound floats out to him from the mountain gorges.

If the hearer have the courage of his curiosity, and will *explore* the sound, his eyes will share the astonishment and consternation of his ears.

It is well, however, to cultivate secretiveness. Woe to him if in seeing he shall be seen ! A sharp-edged knife or flint shall be over-curious of his back, and across its bloody autograph a hundred fearful lashes shall lift their purpling wales—in barbarous hint to him henceforth to keep a curb between the teeth of inquisitiveness.

But let him stalk his game, and with safety to his own hide he may see havoc to the hides of others. In advance a tall, athletic *pitero*, torturing that unearthly unmelody from his rude reed *pito*, and recognizable as one of the leading musicians of the neighborhood. A few rods behind, two other natives bearing lanterns before the feet of the astounding figure which follows them—a head loosely but securely wrapped in a black bag like a hangman's cap ; a body naked to the waist, and clothed below with not more than a pair of flapping linen drawers, now wet with red ; bare feet purple with the savage cold of a New Mexican March, yet not too frozen to bleed responsive to the attentions of the frozen rocks ; and arms which swing mechanically up and back at each step, and bring a broad, plaited whip down upon the macerated back with a heavy swash. A few rods more to the rear

comes another man, in the same fantastic undress, but
without the whip. He staggers under an enormous
cross, its rear end crunching on the rocks and snow
twenty feet behind, its weight five times that of its
bearer. And slowly, painfully, with bleeding backs and
feet and freezing bodies, the self-made martyrs with
their solemn attendants file past the trembling watcher
and disappear among the querulous pines, through
whose arches the tootle of the fife floats fitfully back.

Each Friday night of Lent these strange spectres
flit through the loneliest mountain gorges, until Holy
Week; and then the whipping goes on nightly—but
still in privacy. It is not until Holy Thursday that
the scattered knots of fanatics come together in some
spot where they have a *morada* (brotherhood house),
and do their penance by daylight where the curious
may see without danger to life or limb.

The hamlet of San Mateo—a straggling procession
of brown adobes at the very foot of the mesa foundation of Mount Taylor, at an altitude of nearly eight
thousand feet—contains four hundred people. It is
perhaps the most unreclaimed Mexican village in New
Mexico. Not half a dozen of its people speak the
language of the United States. In 1887 a witch was
stoned to death there, who had played the cynical
trick of turning an estimable citizen into a woman for
the space of three months! Numerous other inhabitants have suffered—though none else so severely—at
the hands of witches; and several in the town have
seen and held converse with his Satanic Majesty!
Little wonder, then, that the dwindling Penitentes
have still kept a foothold there, or that the population
is in awed and active sympathy with their brutalities.

Half a mile along the crazy road which wanders up
into the cañon, whose clear rivulet is the life of the
people, stands the rude little log-built mill, its big,
overshot wheel taking impulse from a monster spout
of pine; its grumbling stones chewing the plump
wheat into a brown, nutritious flour; its madonna-
faced mistress divided between the falling grist and her
toddling babe. Across the road a couple of hundred
yards distant, backed up against a rocky bluff, the
morada's gloomy walls glower down upon the pretty
scene. It is a low, rude hut of stone, some forty by
twenty feet in exterior dimensions, with one door,
two small windows, and two rooms divided by a narrow hallway. The rough walls are unchinked, the
floor is of earth. There are neither chairs, benches,
tables, nor beds; nothing but two of the quaint New
Mexico corner fireplaces, and a few pegs in the wall,
from which depend the whips, stained and stiff with
dry blood. Against the outer walls lean four rude
crosses. The largest is twenty feet long, and weighs
close upon eight hundred pounds; the smallest two
hundred. A few hundred yards down the cañon, a
sugar-loaf hillock, known as *El Calvario*, elbows the
road. Upon its top stands another large cross—the
scene of former crucifixions.

I had been watching feverishly for Holy Week to
come. No photographer had ever caught the Penitentes with his sun-lasso,* and I was assured of death
in various unattractive forms at the first hint of an attempt. But when the ululation of the *pito* filled the
ear at night, enthusiasm crowded prudence to the
wall. The village air grew heavy with mysterious

* Nor has any other yet.

whisperings and solemn expectancy. Whatever they talked about, the people were evidently thinking of nothing else. I wandered through fields and arroyos at all hours of night, trying to trail that mysterious whistle whose echoes seemed to come from all points of the compass ; but in vain. My utmost reward was a glimpse of three ghostly figures just disappearing inside Juanito's house on the hill.

But at last March 29th came around, and with it Holy Thursday. At nine A.M. the shrilling of the *pito* close at hand called us out of the house in haste ; but already the three responsible Penitentes had vanished in the tall chaparral. We greased the rattling buckboard, and hurried over to the village. Every one was out, but they were no longer the friendly *paisanos* we had known. The sight of the camera-box and tripod provoked ominous scowls and mutterings on every hand. Nine-tenths of the population were clustered in close, listless groups along a little wart of houses upon a hill which overhangs the *campo santo* (burying-ground), at the upper end of town. Squatting with backs against the 'dobe walls, the men rolled cigarettes from corn-husks or brown paper, and talked intermittently. The women nursed their babes unconstrainedly, and rolled brown-paper or corn-husk cigarettes. I stowed the obnoxious instrument inside a friendly house, and waited. Waiting seems natural in a Mexican town. The minutes loafed into hours ; and still the talking, the nursing, the smoking went on. Nobody thought of moving.

It was two P.M. when a stir in the crowd on the hill-top told us that *it* was coming at last ; and the camera was straightway planted behind the adobe

THE PENITENTE PROCESSION.

ramparts of the door-yard. In five minutes more a
fifer came over the ridge, followed by five women
singing hymns; and behind them a half-naked figure
with bagged head, swinging his deliberate whip,
whose *swish, thud! swish, thud!* we could hear
plainly two hundred yards away, punctuating the
weird music. In measured step the pilgrims paced
along the reeling footpath, and disappeared around a
spur toward the *morada.* Half an hour later the fife
again asserted itself up the cañon; and soon reap-
peared with its persecutor, the singing women and
the lone self-torturer. As he passed on to the graveyard, we saw that little red rivulets were beginning
to stain the white of his *calzoncillos.*

I hurried to the hill-top, to get near enough for a
" shot ; " but the mob, hitherto only scowling, was
now openly hostile, and I would have fared ill but for
the prompt action of Don Ireneo Chaves, whose reck-
less bravery—a proverb in all that country of brave
men—none cared to provoke. With two stanch,
well-armed friends, he held back the evil-faced mob,
while the instantaneous plates were being snapped
at the strange scene below.

Suddenly another fifer came over the hill, followed
by more women, and seven Penitentes. Of the latter,
four were whipping themselves, and three staggered
under crosses of crushing weight. Slowly and solemnly they strode down the slope to the stone-walled
graveyard, filed through the roofed entrance, whipped
themselves throughout all the paths, knelt in prayer
at each grave, kissed the foot of the central board
cross, and filed out again. These services lasted
twenty minutes. The foremost cross-carrier, after

leaving the graveyard a few rods behind, fell face
down under his fearful load, and lay there with the
great cross-arm resting upon his neck. One of the
Hermanos de Luz (" Brothers of Light," who do not
castigate themselves, but act as attendants upon those
who do) took a whip and gave him fifty resounding
blows on the bare back. Then two *ayudantes* lifted
him to his feet, laid the great timbers upon his neck,
and steadied the ends as he tottered onward. Once
he was about to sink again, but they revived him with
emphatic kicks. So the ghastly procession crept
thrice from *morada* to *campo santo* and back.

At seven o'clock that night the fanatic band came
marching down to the hospitable house of Colonel
Manuel Chaves, the most extraordinary Indian fighter
New Mexico ever produced. A little family chapel
stands a few rods from the house, behind two sturdy
oaks, in whose never-forgotten shade Colonel Chaves
rested one awful day fifty-eight years ago, when,
sieved by seven Navajo arrows, he was crawling his
bloody one hundred and fifty miles homeward to
Cebolleta. Hither the procession turned. There
were now five *Hermanos Disciplinantes*, but only one
of them was using his whip—a short, youthful-seem-
ing fellow of beautiful muscular development. Kneeling in turn and kissing the rude cross that leaned
against one of the trees, each one waddled on his
knees into the chapel and up to the altar, where all
remained kneeling. Back of them were two-score
women on their knees, while a dozen men stood rev-
erently along the wall. The *Hermano Mayor*, José
Salazar—a small, amiable-looking shrivel—raised his
cracked voice in a hymn ; and the audience followed,

in the nasal drawl so dear to native New Mexican
singers. It was an impressive sight—the little adobe
room, whose flaring candles struggled vainly with the
vagrant shadows; the altar bright with chromos of
the saints, a plaster image of the Holy Mother dressed
in tulle and wreaths of paper flowers; the black-
capped, bare-backed five before the altar; and the
awe-struck crowd behind—as they sang over and
over, with intense feeling, if with scant harmony:

" LAS COLUMNAS.*

" En una columna atado
    Hallarás al Rey del Cielo,
Herido y ensangrentado
    Y arrastrado por el suelo.

" En agriesta disciplina,
    Si lo quieres aliviar,
Llega, alma, á desagrabiar
    A la Paloma Divina.

" Ay, Jesús! Ay, mi dulce dueño,
    Desagrabiar te queremos.
Recibe, poder amoroso,
    Las flores de este misterio."

* THE COLUMNS (CROSSES).

"Upon a column bound
    Thou'lt find the King of Heaven,
Wounded and red with blood
    And dragged along the ground.

In bitter discipline
    If thou would'st ease his pain,
Draw nigh, O soul, to give
    Peace to the dove divine.

Alas, Jesus! Alas, my sweet master,
    We long to aid Thee!
Receive, thou loving power,
    The flowers of this mystery."

The Spanish is lame.

Then, at a signal from the *Hermano Mayor*, the
penitent five fell prone upon their faces, with arms
stretched at full length beyond their heads ; and thus
they lay, motionless as death, for three-quarters of an
hour, while the singing, with its fife accompaniment,
still went on.

The services over, the Penitentes filed over to the
house for supper—which dare not be refused them,
even in that cultivated family. The *Hermanos de
Luz* had already effectually blinded the windows ;
and the five active members, filing into the room,
locked the door and plugged the keyhole before they
dared remove their head-masks to eat. This care to
keep their identity secret is observed out of a fear for
the Church. Still, the sympathizing villagers know
pretty surely who each one is.

No one was allowed in the dining-room save the
five self-whippers ; and now came my golden opportunity. Metaphorically collaring the *Hermano
Mayor*, the *Hermanos de Luz*, and the *pitero*, I
dragged them to my room, overwhelmed them with
cigars and other attentions, showed and gave them
pictures of familiar scenes—a Mexican finds it hard to
resist a picture—and cultivated their good graces in
all conceivable ways. And when the Brothers of the
Whip had supped, re-masked themselves and emerged,
the Chief Brother and the Brothers of Light were
mine.

On the morning of Good Friday, March 30, I was
in the village bright and early; and so was every one
else for twenty miles around. At ten o'clock the
Mexican schoolmaster and another prominent citizen
started up the cañon with me, helping to "pack" my

impedimenta. Coming to a point in the road opposite the *morada*, they sat down, refusing to go nearer, and I had to carry the load alone to a hillock a
couple of hundred feet southeast of the house, where
I set up the camera.

Soon the procession hove in sight, coming from
town. Ahead strode the fifer, proudly fingering his
diabolical instrument; then came two *hermanos* with
crosses, and another whipping himself, with half a
dozen *Hermanos de Luz* attending them; then shriv-
eled old Jesus Mirabal reading prayers aloud; and
behind him fifty-one women and children, falling down
on their knees in the dust-deep road at every fifty feet
or so to pray, and singing hymns as they walked between prayers. They bore a large crucifix with the
figure of the Redeemer—strange to say, dressed in a
linen gown—a plaster image of the Holy Virgin, and
numerous framed chromos of the saints. Tallest
among the women was the Mexican wife of the Pres-
byterian missionary then stationed at San Mateo—a
cynical commentary on our mission work.

Reaching the *morada* in their deliberate march, the
Penitentes laid down their crosses and went inside;
the women knelt on the ground before the door and
kept up their singing and praying, while the Brothers
of Light strode here and there with airs of great re-
sponsibility. The ill-faced mob gathered about me,
with unpromising looks, and with significant lumps
beneath their coats. But just then my lonely guard
was relieved by Juan Baca, one of the *Hermanos de
Luz*, who came over from the *morada* swelled with
importance, and whispered most gratifying news.
The *Hermano Mayor* had pondered my request.

After dinner he would hold the procession while I made a picture! So back went the camera into its box, which Juan carried into the *morada*, and back fell the puzzled mob. Presently the procession was renewed, and I marched beside it to dinner.

Now there were three Brothers using the lash, and two carrying crosses; while two more strode unconcernedly along, each with a burro-load of *entraña* (buckhorn cactus) lashed upon his naked back. The *entraña* is one of the most depraved of all its diabolical family. Its spines are long, slenderer and sharper than the sharpest needle, yet firm enough to penetrate any ordinary boot. Get one *entraña* needle into the hide of a steer, and the maddened animal will gallop bellowing over the landscape till it falls from exhaustion. Yet these two fanatics wore huge bundles of it, held on by half-inch hempen ropes drawn so tightly about chest and arms and waist that they cut the skin and stopped the circulation; each must have had thousands of the thorns burrowing into his flesh, but he gave no sign. There was no sham about it. Don Ireneo cut a big *entraña* antler from beside the road, and threw it upon one of them as he passed. The cruel needles pierced his shoulder so deeply that the heavy branch *hung* there, yet he never winced nor turned his head! At the foot of Calvary the procession stopped, while the two men with crosses prostrated themselves in the dust—the crosses being placed upon their backs—and lay thus for ten minutes, the fife and the singers keeping up their discord the while. Every hour of the day these pilgrimages were made between the *campo santo* and the *morada*—a full third of a mile each way.

Shortly before two o'clock the women returned
from town, " making the stations," and halted in front
of the *morada*. Juan Baca brought forth the camera, and the *Hermano Mayor* marked a spot, about
one hundred feet from the door, where I might stand.
Then he called the Brothers from the house and
formed the procession—the cross-bearers in front,
then the Brothers of the Whip, and then the Brothers
of Light and the women. " 'Sta bueno ? " he asked
through Juan ; and when I replied that it was, he
gave orders that no man should stir a finger until
the pictures were taken.

This ordeal over, the Penitentes retired again inside the *morada ;* and the women started on a fresh
pilgrimage.

I was left to chat a moment with Manuel Martin,
one of the Brothers of Light, and a remarkable
character. He is now said to be over one hundred
years old, but is active as a cat. He has a nineteen-
year-old wife, and frequently walks twenty miles of a
morning to visit his father-in-law, who is forty years
younger than he, but does not look it. Very diminutive, Manuel is still straight as an arrow, and remarkably strong. They relate in the village that he used
to kill a sheep with a single blow of his fist—a great
feat for any man. When Manuel lived at Puerto de
Luna he was a shepherd, and used to vegetate with
his flock a year at a time, on wages of $15 per
month. At the end of the year he would return, get
his money—and spend every cent of it in giving the
whole town a grand ball that night !

" And how passes the time ? " I asked the old
man.

7

"*Válgame Dios, Señor,*" he answered; "but I am not well. I saw a strange and woful sight last night. One of the Brothers lay sick in the *morada*, and I was caring for him. At midnight I heard the whistle of Brothers coming from the mountains, and went out. I knelt at meeting them, as is our custom, and when I looked I saw that their feet were bared of flesh—nothing but little white bones. Then I looked up, and saw only two skeletons, whipping themselves upon the naked bones of their backs—and I ran away, crossing myself. *Quizás* they were Brothers who had broken their vows and now must wander without rest."

Meantime other *Hermanos de Luz*, including Juan Baca and "Cuate" — the cleverest wrestler in the Territory, despite his years—had burrowed out a deep hole some fifty feet in front of the *morada*, and laid the largest cross with its foot at the edge of the hole. The procession of women had returned, and stood solemnly in front of the hundreds of spectators. And now the *Hermano Mayor* went into the *morada* with two of his assistants. In a few moments they emerged leading the allotted victim, a stalwart young fellow dressed only in his white drawers and black head-bag. As we learned later, it was Santiago Jaramillo—known also as "Santiago Jeems"—the cook at the house of Don Roman A. Baca, one of the sheep-kings of the Territory. In his right side was a gaping gash four inches long, from which the blood ran down to the ground in a steady stream. He walked firmly to the prostrate cross, however, and laid himself at full length upon it. A long, new, half-inch rope was brought, and the *Hermanos de Luz* be-

gan to lash him to the great timbers, placing the stiff
hemp around his arms, trunk, and legs in three or
four loops each, and " cinching up " the slack as un-
gently as they would upon a pack-mule. He was
sobbing like a child, "*Ay! Como estoy deshonrado!*
Not with a rope! Not with a rope! Nail me! Nail
me!" But the *Hermano Mayor* was obdurate. Always before, up to this very year, the victim had been
nailed to the cross by great spikes through hands and
feet, and the death of a Penitente during the crucifixion was by no means rare. But the new *Hermano
Mayor*, a more intelligent and humane man than his
predecessors, and also perchance with more of the
fear of the church before his eyes, drew the line at
nails, despite the appeals of the victim not to be dis-
honored by a lighter agony.

He fared badly enough, as it was. The stiff rope
sank deep into his flesh and prohibited the throbbing
blood. In less than three minutes his arms and legs
were black as a Hottentot's. A clean white sheet
was now wound about him from head to foot and tied
there, leaving exposed only his purpling arms and
muffled head. This was done, so one of the attendants explained to me, that no sharp-eyed bystander
might recognize him by scars on his body. Now the
rope was knotted to the arms of the cross, so that
each end hung free and about thirty feet long. Two
stalwart Brothers of Light grasped each end; four
others seized the cross; and heavily they lifted it so
near to perpendicularity that the lower end dropped
into the four-foot hole with an ugly *chug!* But its living burden made no sign. With shovels and hands
the assistants filled in the hole with earth and rocks,

and stamped it down, while a stout fellow steadied
each guy-rope.

A large rock was next placed five feet from the foot
of the cross, and another Penitente in cotton drawers
and headbag was led out, with a huge stack of cactus
so tightly lashed upon his back that he could not
move his hands at all, and scarcely his legs. He lay
down with his feet against the cross and his head pil-
lowed upon the stone, while the mass of *entraña* kept
his back sixteen or eighteen inches above the ground.
Even this was not a tight enough fit to suit him, and
he had a large flat stone brought and crowded under
the cactus, so as to press it still more cruelly against
his back.

Meantime, in gracious response to my request, the
Hermano Mayor had paced off thirty feet from the
foot of the cross, that I might come nearer and get a
larger picture. And there we stood facing each other,
the crucified and I—the one playing with the most
wonderful toy of modern progress, the other racked
by the most barbarous device of twenty centuries
ago.

For thirty - one minutes by the watch the poor
wretch upon the cross and he on the bed of thorns
kept their places. A deathly hush was upon the
crowd. Even the unwilling *pito* was still. The
millstream spilt its music upon the rough old wheel,
now locked and unresponsive. The fresh breeze
rustled among the piñons on the steep mountain-
side a few rods away. The undimmed afternoon
sun flooded the rugged cañon with strange glory.
Across the brook a chubby prairie dog, statuesquely
perpendicular, watched the ghastly scene and barked

JUAN BACA.   JESUS MIRABAL.   JOSE SALAZAR,   FILOMENO.   CISTO.   "CUATE."   'MELITO.
HERMANO MAYOR,

CRUCIFIXION OF A PENITENTE, SAN MATEO, N. M., MARCH 30, 1888.

his creaking disapprobation—the only animate sound
that reached the ear. Near the cross stood the old
Hermano Mayor, and beside him Manuel, Juan, Philomeno, " Cuate," Victorio, Melito. Each had a narrow fillet of wild rose branches bound tightly around
his skull. Coming nearer, I saw that the claw-like
thorns were forced deep into the skin, and that little
crimson beads stood out upon each forehead.

At last the Chief Brother spoke a quiet word. The
assistants scooped out the dirt from the hole, lifted
the cross from its earthen socket, and laid it upon
the ground again. The crucified was relieved of his
lashings, was lifted to his feet, and carried to the *morada*, a stout *paisano* under each shoulder, while his
feet made feeble feint of moving. His brother victim
was similarly taken in with his worse than Nessus-
robe; and the procession re-formed for its awful pilgrimages, which were kept up till six o'clock. As
we walked down the cañon beside the procession,
forcibly obliged to stop every time it halted to pray,
I had leisure to study the peculiar marching-step of
the Penitentes.

The cross bearers stagger as best they may under
such fearful burdens, but the whippers have a strange
step from which they never vary. Each man stands
with his muffled head drooping almost upon his chest,
his left hand held upon his right nipple, and his right
hand grasping the heavy whip. Shoving his right
foot slowly forward to the length of an ordinary step,
he plants it with a smart slap, at the same time swinging his right arm upward and backward so that the
long, broad lash strikes upon the left side of the back
at " the small." Thus he pauses full two seconds,

the lash resting upon the raw flesh ; then shoves his left foot forward, while bringing his whip back in front of him, and with another stamp swishes the whip over upon the right side of his back. By this time of day their drawers were wet with blood behind to the very ankles. One *Hermano de Luz* carried a tin-pail containing a decoction of *romero*, and every two or three minutes dipped the ends of the " *disciplinas* " in this, to give them an additional sting.

The whips are about three and a half feet long, and weigh about two pounds. They are made of the tough fibres of the *palmilla ;* * whose saponaceous root (the familiar *amole*) serves the New Mexican housewife in lieu of soap, and whose rosettes of emerald daggers dot these arid uplands. The handle is braided ; and the lash, a couple of feet long and three to five inches across, is left to bristle like the tail of a horse. This is the " *disciplina* " of penance. To punish erring members they have the " *disciplina* of castigation "—a hideous cat-o'-nine-tails made of wire, with the ends turned up claw-fashion, so that every blow ravishes from the back its tiny morsels of flesh.

As we passed Calvary again, a new horror was added. The *Hermano Mayor* came up behind each of the seven self-torturers, and with a flint knife gashed their backs thrice across and then " crosshatched " them thrice up and down. They were no mere scratches, but long, bleeding cuts. This is the official seal of the order, and is annually renewed.

At eight o'clock in the evening the procession came down again from the *morada*, this time marching the length of the town to hold *tinieblas* (dark services)

* *Yucca baccata.*

in the little chapel next to the house of Don Lorenzo
Sanchez. The Penitentes went inside and barred the
door on the crowd. There were no lights within, and
the windows were carefully shuttered. All that came
to the shivering audience outside was the clanking of
chains and muffled blows, and groans and shrieks.
The services—which are intended to represent the
arrival of the soul in purgatory—lasted an hour.
Then the Penitentes emerged, carrying one of their
number in a blanket held by the corners. We learned
afterward that he had hugged a stake wrapped with
cactus for fifteen minutes, and had succumbed to this
fresh torture. Around him plodded seven women,
weeping bitterly, but low. Not one but feared it
was her own husband. The poor wretch lay long
at death's door, but finally recovered.

One short, stocky fellow, who had been particularly
zealous in his blows all day, and who had lain upon
the thorns at the foot of the cross, attracted my particular attention; and walking back from the chapel
to the plaza, a third of a mile, I kept at his side and
counted the blows he gave himself—two hundred and
fifty-one. During the day he had laid on over two
thousand; and heaven only knows how many before;
but next day he was at work with his irrigating hoe.
He is a young man, Antonito Montaño by name, and
not easy of suppression. A mule once caved in
his face, and a soldier in a drunken quarrel gave him
grounds for being trepanned; but he is still keen to
enjoy such tortures as the most brutal prize-fighter
never dreamed of.

At midnight of Good Friday, the Penitentes scattered from the *morada* toward their homes—in some

cases forty miles away—to meet no more in a religious capacity until another Lent.   By their incredible
self-torture, one would naturally suppose them to be
the most God-fearing and devout of men, but this
would be a serious error.   There are among them
good but deluded men, like the *Hermano Mayor*,
Salazar and Cuate ; but many of them are of the low-
est and most dangerous class—petty larcenists, horse-
thieves, and assassins, who by their devotions during
Lent think to expiate the sins of the whole year.   The
brotherhood, though broken, still holds the balance
of political power.   No one likes—and few dare—to
offend them ; and there have been men of liberal edu-
cation who have joined them to gain political influence.   In fact it is unquestionable that the outlawed
order is kept alive in its few remote strongholds by
the connivance of wealthy men, who find it convenient
to maintain these secret bands for their own ends.

On the night of October 17, 1888, a political
meeting was held in the *morada* at San Mateo,
at the call of a prominent young man there, since
an embezzler and refugee from justice, whose edu-
cation at Georgetown and other Eastern universities cost his fond father $36,000.   The county cam-
paign was very close ; and finding that he was losing
ground, the young man called upon the Penitentes to
assist him.   He was at that meeting initiated into the
order, and received its seal—six gashes with the flint
knife over each kidney.   The wife of this young politician, by the way, is the daughter of a prominent
Washington official, recently deceased.   It may also
be added that a Penitente was crucified in San Mateo
on Good Friday, 1889, 1890, and 1891.

Until recently there were also female Penitentes; and up to 1886 there dwelt in San Mateo fully ten women who whipped their bare backs, wore cactus thorns in their loose shoes, and wound their legs with ropes and wire till the blood stopped—practices which still obtain among the men. Other common forms of penance are to lie down before the church and request worshippers to walk over them and kick them; or to crawl on hands and knees along a path paved with cactus.

The Penitentes have a manuscript book of rules, but it is impossible for an outsider to get hold of a copy. Some of these laws are well-known, however. One of their most curious customs is that regarding burial. When a brother is taken sick, he is removed to the *morada* and cared for by a member appointed by the *Hermano Mayor*, no one else being permitted to see him. If he dies, the Brothers wrap him naked in a blanket and secretly bury him at 1 A.M., feet down in a deep hole in some secluded spot. His clothes are then left at his home—the first and final token his family has of his decease, and perhaps even of his sickness. No married man, by the way, is allowed to join the order without the consent of his wife.

Sins against the property, families, or lives of persons outside the order, are taken no cognizance of whatever, but if a Penitente injure a brother in any of these points, his punishment is severe. The laws of the land are not acknowledged, but the *Hermano Mayor* sentences the offender according to the gravity of his crime, to be scourged with the terrific wire whip, to be buried to the neck all night in a gigantic *olla* (water-jar) or to be interred completely, alive and forever. I was informed on good Friday that Philomeno had been buried up to his neck all the night before for beating his wife. For betraying the secrets of the order, the standard punishment is to be buried alive. The law does not trouble the executors of these extra-judicial sentences. The Brothers merely give out that the victim has left the country ; and they have taken good care that it shall be impossible to prove the contrary.

In collecting the songs and *dichos* of the native population of the Territory, I have come across one irreverent verse relating to the Penitentes.   It runs :

> " Penitente pecador,
>   Porque te andas azotando ?
>   Por una vaca que robé
>   Y aqui la ando disquitando."

Which is, by interpretation,

> Penitente sinner,
>   Why do you go whipping yourself ?
> " For a cow that I stole,
>   And here I go paying for her."

V

THE CHASE OF THE CHONGO

THE CHASE OF THE CHONGO

AFTER the Spring medicine-making has set the
year afoot in the paths of safety ; and five hundred swart spade-bearers have turned a sample of the
Rio Grande down the "mother-canal" whose little
daughter-ditches shall feed the parched fields ; and
they who will not come out and dance for this drink-
giving that the wheat and corn may spring, have been
duly ducked for their contumacy, then is it that my
brown friends of the pueblo of Isleta have joy of their
legs. And joy shall be as well to all who see ; for
never was there more gallant sight than the running
of the stark and sinewy forty when they chase the
elusive chongo.*

In the abstract, the Pueblo is far from the supreme
runner. The Apache or the Mojave, given three
days' time, could fairly circumnavigate him. But as
compared with anything familiar to our putative athletics, he is peerless—naturally enough, for he has not
yet degenerated into the fulness of civilization. Our
record-breakers would be record-broken were they
entered in the *Nah-cui-e-wee* of the spring in Isleta.

I have said that the Indian does nothing for fun ;
nor does he primarily. But he has achieved the precious ability to squeeze fun from duty. He even runs
for God's sake, but trusts no offence will be taken if

---

* The Egyptian queue in which both sexes dress their hair.

he shall be as glad therein as his deity. He feels
there is room for both. The coming of spring brings
a host of sacred ceremonials, whereof the relay foot-
race is not most potent but by far most picturesque.

The races always begin on Easter Sunday afternoon, and generally last four Sundays. They are in
honor of the Cacique, the vicar of Thoor-íd-deh, the
Sun-Father ; and if he have in him half the blood of
a man, those twenty hours pay him for all the self-
abnegation of the year.

At noon of Easter, Desiderio Jaramillo, the superb
War-Captain, is afoot in the uncertain streets of the
Pueblo, *pregonando* in a voice that Stentor's self
might envy. Seven years have not dulled my wonder at the sonorous range of Pueblo throats. Slow,
measured, deep, resonant, his voice rolls down the
breathless air in glorious baritone :

HÁH-TAH ö'-wun toó-hlahk
mah-eé-kah !

" Now, youths, to the estufa come ! "

To-day is the day of the smalls. In half an hour
after Desiderio has bombarded the town with those
explosive thunders of his chest, men of age begin
trudging toward the low, round estufa, leading each
his smaller copy. By one o'clock the twilit room is
crowded with old men and ungrown boys. All come
who wish—none are barred. To them rises the Cacique in benediction ; and the Captain of War pro-
claims that now is the time when the pueblo shall try
its runners, if they have the hearts of men, and teach
the youth to bear their course, that they be strong if
ever shall come the *barbaros*. Then he names two

old men present as captains for the day, and they proceed to "choose sides" in the fashion of "picking up" two base-ball nines. " I choose Quico," says the first grayhead. " And I Lelo," says the other. And so they pick alternately until all the lads present are arrayed upon one side or the other. Then are marked those of the first side, each with a dab of *yeso* on his right cheek; and all strip off their moccasins and muslin trousers and gay print shirts, and stand slender and supple in no more than the modest breech-clout.

By four o'clock the plaza has usurped the town. Upon the wall before the great, gray adobe church— which dates from before 1635—is perched a long row of the expectant. Upon the squat roofs which wall the three other sides of the square, is the rest of the population. The course is diagonally across the plaza; and the two goals, one hundred and sixty yards apart, are marked by the statuesque elders who shall judge the race.

And now a hush befalls the crowd. From the tortuous little alley at the southwest corner of the plaza stalks Desiderio, swathed in a priceless blanket of the weavers who never wash. Behind him, with pace as stately, strides a gracile lad of twelve, and another, and another, until a procession of thirty boys in single file, tapering downward to the centre and then up again, and brought up as to the rear by a man with silver locks, is marching across the plaza. The oldest may be thirteen; the tiniest is not to exceed five. But their hearts are the hearts of strong men.

To the farther goal they march, and wheel and stand for a brief invocation. Then half remain there, and the rest file back to the western goal.

A moment's pause, and the command rings out like a pistol shot; and with the word two of them that are at the eastern goal leap forward like twin arrows from a single bow. They are the largest boys of the thirty. One is of the Ee-too-in, with the *yeso* print; the other of the Ee-áh-too ín, that wear no paint. Like two fawns they spring down the course, and in a flash of lithe brown legs they are at the hither goal, and their two next mates, a painted and an unpainted, are springing to the east. Each pair is smaller than the one before it, till five-year-old Melito and chubby Juan, a year his senior, are legging it with unbound hair out-blown, set lips, and eyes afire. What strain of dimpled legs, what play of baby-chests, what spread of young nostrils that sniff the breath of victory!

The Pueblo foot-race is a serial athletic in many chapters. From goal to goal is not a race—it is not even, strictly speaking, a heat. The race is by relays and cumulative, and the fortunes of the two sides are as a bank-account whereto are debited and credited the loss or gain of the successive representatives of each. The start is always from the eastward goal, and by one runner of each side. If they reach the western goal even, the second pair start even toward the east. Generally one is a little ahead; and in such case, his mate starts from the goal the instant he reaches it, thus preserving for his side the gain made by its first man. The second man of the other side cannot start out till *his* man comes in. In other words, the result is like that of a straight-away race of forty miles or so between two men, each of whom is made new and fresh at every few hundred yards.

CHASE OF THE CHONGO.

The race of the babies is not apt to last long. Each of the fifteen of each side runs his one hundred and sixty yards three or four times in his turn; and at last one is plucked from behind by his rival between goals, and the race is over. The next Sunday's race, similarly announced, is between two parties of grown men, similarly chosen. They are generally young; though now and then an elder pants his course, in payment of some votive debt to Those Above for his recovery from sickness. There are generally in these races but eight or ten men on a side; so the running is apt to be long without result, since each man has to run oftener and has less time to rest. Frequently a race is not finished by sunset; in which case it goes over bodily till the next Sunday, when the gaining side will start in ahead by the exact number of feet it has won from the other.

But it is when the specific races of the Cacique have been run, that the climax comes. By now the blood of old and young is warm with rivalry. Four afternoons they have watched that brave and generous strife, with gathering unrest, till now their spirits can be appeased only by running themselves. No sooner is the chongo of the unpainted unfortunate begrappled, than friendly taunt and challenge are bandied from mouth to mouth of them that surge toward the estufa with the victorious painted. Before the sacred council-room is gained, a formal *défi* has passed. The unmarried men challenge the benedicts to a foot-race on the coming Sunday.* This looks

---

* Occasionally the challenge is from those whose farms are across the river to those on this side; and, more rarely yet, the parties are sometimes made up from the dwellers on either side of an imaginary north and south line drawn through the middle of the plaza.

more like pure fun—but still the ceremonial heart is in it. The bet is a scalp-dance! The side which loses shall pay the dance—that is, trudge with unhasteful burros to the Manzanos, twenty miles away, and bring back wood for the great bonfire without which no *Tu-a-fú-ar* can be held. The challenge is of course accepted—it would be simply impossible, under Indian etiquette, to be "stumped." The race will be exactly like its predecessors, "only more so;" and because this most superb of athletics takes climax with its last race, I have reserved detailed description for that.

That same night, after sunset, there are rallyings to two points. Upon a broom-peak of the gathered house-sweepings of five hundred years, in the eastern part of the pueblo, cluster Hlóo-hlin, the "Old Men" or married; and "O-wun," the single, flock to a similar mound west of the plaza. Each party elects a captain, and he carefully picks his men. Every night through the week the rival bands meet, each at its rendezvous, and chant loudly to the tap of the rawhide drum, and train on a level street. As practice goes on, and lungs broaden and legs evict their kinks, spirits bubble over. To-night the *Casados* come parading past the camp of the *Solteros*, headed by the vociferous drum, waving a gorgeous banner and singing in mighty chorus an improvised Tigua war-song of which the literal translation is:

> " Day after to-morrow
> How strong we will run !
> How we will gain on,
> How we will chase you,
> Catching by the *chongo*,
> Tearing off the breech-clout !

All of the meal-pay,
All of the flour-pay,
Girls, go and hide it !
So when the Solteros
Lose in the running,
There shall be nothing—
Nothing to pay them ! "

This, with the appreciative titter of buxom married women on a hundred listening housetops is ill to be borne ; but the young bachelors are equal to the occasion.   Troubadours are no rarity here ; and to-morrow night the youths take banner and *tombé* and march past the rendezvous of the married, singing strongly :

" Ho ! what are old men ?
Good to hobble burros !
Good for burro-drivers!
Good for drinking *vino !*
Crooked are their *chongos !*
How they hug the fireplace !
So much the Hloo-hlin,
Nothing else they're good for ! "

By Sunday noon the town is in a high fever. Every man, woman, and child of it has espoused a side ; everyone brims with praises of his or her favorites.   There is like to be such running as was never before in the chief home of the Tiguas.   Anywhere else these tense nerves would mean a row to come—anywhere but among these whose nerves have never lost their elasticity for the strain of civilized worry.   The excitement almost over-topples the conventions ; and sweet-faced maidens smile openly back to sinewy youth whose glance they would evade demurely at any other time.   Who shall not run his fierce utmost for such beaming eyes, the heart of a man is not in him, nor yet the hurrying blood.

The racers are in the estufa, from either spar of whose lofty ladder flaunt their respective banners. The race-course is farther down the same indeterminate street. I have never been allowed to measure it, but have done so secretly. It is exactly three hundred and twenty yards from goal to goal, each marked by a pole set in the hard earth. The course has been swept scrupulously clean of every loose particle of sand and gravel. It is hard-pan, sown with round pebbles ; a sort of earthen conglomerate. One of our runners would fare ill, barefoot upon that hard track. Isleteño feet suffer too, but that is part of it. To be stoic and to toughen by pain—they are of the aboriginal curriculum.

The houses that hem the course on either side are a double rainbow. Above their soft gray walls the level roofs are lost in a gorgeous human drift. It is the apotheosis of color. Erect men tower statue-like above the crowd of mothers who nurse brown babes, and maidens who whisper and titter. Upon a commanding hillock cluster a hundred men ; and either side of the street of running is six deep with the more feverish. Upon an ancient bench beside the western goal sit the Cacique and his two assistants and the principal shamans, rolling cigarettes in the sweet corn-husk and smoking gravely. Beside either goal stand its two judges, side by side, erect, tireless, impassive.

Now a head rises from the trap-door of the estufa, and the War-Captain steps out upon the roof and descends the old steps to the ground, followed by the swart athletes in single file; and solemnly they march down to the western goal. There are forty-four runners—twenty-two to a side—the unmarried distinguished by the dab of *yeso* upon the cheek. Desi-

A WATCHER OF THE RACE.

derio heads the procession, and his first sub-captain brings up its rear. The seated dignitaries have risen and taken their places in two files behind the umpires, facing to the east. Down through the aisle between them stalks the procession, while the shamans blow each from his left palm a pinch of the sacred corn-

meal in invocation to Those Above ; and all bow their
heads while the Cacique prays the prayer of the running.

Then the whole procession strides away to the
east goal, and the officials resume their seats. There
is another invocation, and there half the runners stay :
and presently the rest, still led by gallant Desiderio,
file back to the western goal. There they take their
places in two single files ; the eleven Solteros ranged
behind their umpire, the eleven married men behind
theirs. It is a fine array, this score of bronze Apollos,
stark but for the dark blue *taparabo* at the loins,
lithe, muscular, alert. They stand in the order in
which they were chosen. Here is big, homely Quico,
the deer-footed ; and beside him as rival huge, clumsy but tireless Tranquilino. Next of the unmarried
stands that bronze cameo Remigio, the absolute per-
fection of a man ; and for his match the taller Apollo,
José Diego with his poet's face. Do not smile at the
notion of a poet's profile on an Indian. If you or I
had such faces as José Diego or princely Pablo yonder, civilization would give us our livelihood for the
privilege of gazing, as it does now to men less en-
dowed. And here is little Chino, the Black Antelope
who runs five hours at the heads of our loping horses
in the great round-hunt ; and here that *chopo* * Her-
cules, Francisco, the strongest man of the Tiguas,
and matchless in breaking bronco horses and wild
steers ; and here Vicente, the tall wrestler ; and a
brave array besides.

There is a moment when none take breath ; the
Capitan thunders a call to the farther goal ; a sonor-

* A short, heavy-set man.

ous echo gives him answer; and from afar we hear the mighty "*hai-koo!*" of the signal, and there is a flash of something from the farther goal. Upon this first *partura* many a pony and many a costly blanket and many a barrel of wine will change hands; for it is between the two swiftest of all Isleta's eleven hundred—one-eyed Quico and the blonde giant José. The calm of the housetops breaks in rainbow waves of excitement. The street itself surges; and high above its kaleidoscopic tide come streaming the opposing banners, borne by fleet and frantic Chirina and transformed Pedro as they fly side by side with their favorites, for a stretch, to cheer them on. And how the shouts go up!

"*Hai-kóo-ee!*" they thunder from behind, and "*Hai-bai!*" "From the East!" we roar as they flash on.

"*Ah-quá-mi-áhm! Ah-quá-mi-áhm!* Harder! Harder!" yell the unmarried, for Quico is a yard to the bad. But there is no harder in him. Flash his one eye as it will, and wing their best his sinewy arms, and toil their mightiest those corded legs, they avail not against that terrible apparition that hurtles in front. For José the yellow-haired is at his prime to-day, and then no man alive can beat him on that course. Four feet ahead of his rival he leaps past the goal in a fearful bound, and sinks upon a patch of soft sand, that those heaving lungs shall catch up with the stampeded heart.

The second man of each side was crouched catlike at the goal as they came; and as José passed the post his relief leaped forward and was off like the wind. An instant later, in came Quico, and simultaneously his mate sprang to pursue José's; and the clamor of vibrant shouts went up again to heaven.

For three hours it goes thus, without apparent slacking of gait, and with a crescendo of enthusiasm. Each man's turn comes about every fifteen minutes, so each has a chance for wind. The married have gained seventy-five yards in a dozen *parturas;* but there the *solteros* hold them; and the two men near each goal who mark the point where man meets man (of opposite sides) have to move but little. But now the married man gains a rod; and the inspiration feathers anew winged feet that seemed before to run all that man can run. And Lelo robs the bachelors of another yard; and Chino steals two; and Remigio another; and the crowd sways to and fro with the resistless contagion of their flight; and old men gird up their loins and pant beside the runners with voices that crack across the " *Ah-nyah-moó-ee !* " and the " *Hoo-yoi-tin !* " And wrinkled mothers totter parallel with sons whose teeth are grimly set. And plump wives and comely virgins patter in modest trot in the course of the stern-faced meteor that flashes past unsmiling, unturning, but noting those dear encouragements, be sure. Even the staid old Governor and his two lieutenants are running and cheering with the best.

Upon the soft sand-patches at either goal are sprawled a dozen stark forms, twisting for rest or lying with high chests heaving from that terrific strain. Old men pinch and squeeze at cramps and knotted legs. A gay tinaja stands near, with a gourd dipper floating in its neck; but no one drinks. Each runner takes a mouthful and holds it in his parched mouth a

moment, and then blows it—Chinese-laundry fashion
—upon the broad, bare back of a companion ; or puffs
it up against the wind and whirls to catch the return-
ing spray upon his own shoulders.   One or two lean
deathly sick against a wall.   But they will be ready
to step to the scratch when their turn comes around
again.

And still the markers are kept on the gallop, draw-
ing ever nearer to each other in mid-course.   And now
they meet, and pass, and with every *partura* each is
working toward the other goal.   And now in a roar of
joy a staring runner of the married comes to the goal
while yet his rival is starting from the other.   The
Casados have gained a whole lap !   They are no longer
common racers, but now inspired beings.   Their bodies
seem transfigured by a superhuman passion.   I have
seen the bravest struggles of the Superior Race—its
hottest foot-ball fights, its wildest races.   I have heard
more noise, for the aborigine is less noisy than we ;
and seen more acrobatics of the multitude.   But never
have I seen, nor do I look to see, in civilization, such
an apocalypse of inspiration.   No man that is born of
woman could more sit still against that wave of impulse than he could out-weary a red-hot stove.   Im-
petus is in the air, and all goes down before it.   For
now it is no longer a race but a pursuit.   From goal
to goal rings the cry " *Ah-shör !* "   Catch !   Each
bachelor speeds as from a pack of wolves ; each *Ca-
sado* springs like a wolf upon his trail.   Neither could
run a hair the better if his life hung on the instant.
They leap along like very demons—as man was
meant to run when there is to run for.   It is the supreme strain of perfect muscle.   The women who

paddle encouragingly up and down could be no more
wrought up did the pursuer bear a knife for the pursued.   It is good, now that single-heartedness is becoming a lost art, when we so seldom see man do
absolutely his last-best, to look upon the Homeric
heroism of an Isleta hair-chase.

The distance grows smaller between each relay,
until it is but fifty feet as Juan gets to the eastern
goal and 'Mingo flashes west.   And now comes Pedro
to that post, and José springs forward in pursuit of
'Mingo.

I would fain back out, even now, from trying to
tell that untellable last dash.   But even as I pelt im-
potent words at that whose very skin they seem not
to graze, the race is with me again, and the gray faces
of the runners, and the devil's tattoo of their mad
feet, and again I am running with them.   Here comes
'Mingo like a doe with the pack at her heels, with
head back and ashen lips, and brown hide that seems
taut all over, and the eyes of one that sees Death
smite him unavenged.   But behind, like a tawny elk
in rutting-time, comes charging that matchless Fate—
the sublimest human thing I have ever seen.   That six
feet of mighty and faultless frame seems alive at every
pore.   The flawless skin is lighter than my hands—for
José is a blond Indian—and knotted with great gnarls
of strength.   The yellow-brown hair flaunts in massy
waves behind.   The large eyes fairly burn one with
their unearthly glow.   The face is drawn till the skin
is as a drum-head, and the large white teeth flash from
between tense lips.   I trust the frontier has not made
me unduly timorous ; but that desperate face will always haunt me.   It even now and then sets me to

dreaming—a lost art for these fifteen years. It is the
incarnation of do or die, literally, and *now*. None
who sees it may doubt that this is the last *partura*.
José will catch-by-the-hair, unless the world ends before yonder goal.

'Mingo is ashen as the gray track, but with every
rod desperation seems to lend new wings. But they
count not against that human whirlwind that sweeps
and leaps behind in terrific menace, devouring the
course, defying time. 'Mingo can hear the snort of
the great lungs, the pat of the inevitable feet; and
in an instant more, in stone's-throw of safety and the
farther goal, a mighty hand clutches him by the flying chongo—and all is up.

The crowd closes in upon victors and vanquished;
and hoarse throats shout again, and faces are aflame,
and here and there are tears in gentle eyes as the tide
sweeps on to the estufa. Into its cavernous depths
plunge the four-and-forty runners, and rub themselves
and don the garb of every day. The unmarried seek
their homes by the shortest cut; but the victorious
Casados with drum and banner make circuit of the
town, singing loudly of victory. José, the victor-
in-chief, waves aloft his spoils—the banner of the
Öwun, now hung upon with a wreath of the sacred
gold-flower that flecks the gravel-bank beside the
river. For all those hours of supreme effort, they
still have legs and lungs left to celebrate their
victory.

While they are yet parading, a tall and stately
woman dressed in her costliest, rounds a corner of the
plaza, bearing upon her head a flaring Apache basket
covered with a spotless cloth. She is the wife of

José. Behind her come his mother and sisters and a
hundred and twenty other women, each similarly
head-laden. In single file—and there are few more
charming pictures than such a party of Pueblo women
in holiday attire—they proceed to the house of poor
'Mingo, whose queue was pulled. All are sorry for
the loser of that brave strife. There is no reward
for the winner, save glory ; but to him who was
caught goes a most generous consolation - prize.
Since he is a Soltero, every married woman in the
town—and, very like, many a sympathizing maiden
too—will bring him the *Nah-hué-mi* of flour and
meal and calico and sugar and meat and other offerings, till his storeroom shall bulge with fatness.
Often this consolation-pay amounts to over $100 in
cash value ; and as a token of the Acadian spirit of
my townsmen, it may be mentioned that I have heard
the whole pueblo congratulating one another that he
who was caught-by-the-hair was a poor boy, and not
one of the *ricos* to whom the gifts would do no good.
And, furthermore, it is noteworthy that this considerable temptation never yet relaxed a poor boy's legs
from supreme effort. None of the gifts go to console
the others of his side ; but he carries to the Cacique
the first basket—that brought by the chief female
representative of the catcher.

The mental balance in all this is one of the things
which breed deep respect for the Pueblo in everyone
who knows him. No crowd of ours could come to
such fever heat without bad blood somewhere be-
trayed. But the Pueblo does not lose his feet, no
matter how his head shall levitate. He can differenti-
ate between the race and the runner, even in his

wildest tension; and his excitement, his love and hate are purely impersonal. He has no faintest suspicion of a grudge for anyone. I shall never forget one old man who had bet his all and was simply frantic with excitement. His feelings carried him away so far that he protruded seriously upon the

DESIDERIO ISLETA, WAR CAPTAIN OF ISLETA.

track. Stalwart Desiderio went and plucked him up and bore him off bodily to one side; and there the old man stood, the picture of woe, still crazy with the race, but never forgetting so far the respect due to

9

authority as to intrude more, or even scowl. And he was not the exception but the unvarying rule.

The giving of the consolation is the last of the races. The flushed crowd scatters to its homes. At eight to-night the vanquished will set torch to their huge bonfire in the plaza; and the Bending Woman will bring out from their hiding-place in the estufa the weathered scalps of the wars of long ago; and around the roaring cedar logs will dance night-long the great, dark ring with songs of how they smote the prowling *barbaros* who swooped upon Isleta in the danger days of the Olds.

VI

THE WANDERINGS OF COCHITÍ

THE WANDERINGS OF COCHITÍ

O F that unique racial chess-playing of the Pueblos, whereof the board was half the size of Europe and the chessmen were stone cities, there is one foremost example—the Quéres pueblo of Cochití. Other towns may very possibly have moved more (and we know of several movings of each one) ; but of it we have the clearest and fullest itinerary—a record of eight distinct consecutive moves, beginning many centuries before history, and ending with the Spanish reconquest in 1694. In that time the Cochiteños successively occupied the most commanding " squares " along a fifty-mile line of one of the most weirdly, savagely picturesque checker-boards in all North America, and one of the least guessed by Caucasians. When we shall have become a little less a nation of mental mistletoes, American tourists and American writers and artists will find, in the wonderful wilderness between the Puyé and the present Cochití, fascinations for eye and pen and brush not inferior to those of the superannuated Mecca abroad. If we could but have had Hawthorne or Ruskin among those noble *potreros* and dizzy gorges ! How either would have interpreted the gray romance of those grim, far days of the cave-house and the town-moving ! For, with all the nobility of the landscape—

which is entirely characteristic, and in its kind not surpassed anywhere—its strongest appeal is to the " human interest." How the first Americans lived and loved and toiled and watched and fought and endured here !

The Cochití upland is a vast and singular plateau in the centre of northern New Mexico, some fifty miles west of Santa Fé. Its average altitude is over seven thousand feet; and along the west it upheaves into the fine Valles range of eleven thousand. Between these peaks and the Rio Grande, a distance of twenty miles, lies the plateau proper—a vast bench, approximately level to the eye, furred with forests, peculiarly digitated by great cañons. It is a characteristically Southwestern formation ; and yet it is distinct from anything else in the Southwest. It is our only country of *potreros*. It is difficult to diagram ; but perhaps the best idea of its ground-plan is to be had by laying the two hands side by side upon a table, with every finger spread to its widest. The Rio Grande flows about north and south through the line of the knuckles, in a gorge over two thousand feet deep. The spread fingers represent the cañons ; the wedge-shaped spaces between them are the tall *potreros*. These vast tongues of volcanic rock—some of trap, some of lava, some of dazzling pumice—a dozen or more miles long, eight to ten in width nearest the mountains, taper to a point at the river, and there break off in columnar cliffs from one thousand to twenty-five hundred feet in height. From the river, the western side of its dark gorge seems guarded by a long, bright line of gigantic pillars. As always, the Spanish nomenclature was aptly descriptive.

Among the noblest of these cliff-pillars are the beetling Chapéro, over whose dire precipices the Cochiteños used to drive their game in the great communal round-hunts; the Potrero del Alamo, a terrific wedge of creamy rock, whose cliffs are nearly two thousand feet tall; and the wildly beautiful Potrero de las Vacas. It is a region of remarkable scenic surprises. Every approach is of enormous roughness; of alternate descent into savage chasms and toiling up precipitous *cumbres*, whose crest flings a sudden and in-

THE STONE PUMAS OF THE POTRERO DE LAS VACAS.

effable vista against the eye. At one's feet, and far below, is the Plan del Rio—the yawning gulf of the Rio Grande—guarded by its western phalanx of *potreros*. To the east and north are the blackened leagues of the Santa Fé plateau, with its small volcanic cones, over which peep the snow-peaks of the coccyx of the Continent—the ultimate vetebræ of the Rockies. To the southeast the jagged peaks of the Ortiz range prick the sky, and the horizon hangs on the round shoulders of the giant Sandia. South are the dim wraiths of the Ladrones, and the silver beads of the river amid its lower fields and cotton-woods. The west is lost behind the dark ranks of the Valles giants, captained by the lonely pyramid of Abiquiu. It is a wonderful picture, and withal an awesome one. Here was the Coliseum of volcanic gladiators.   Trap, basalt, lava, pumice, scoriæ—all is igneous.   And this arson of a landscape has a startling effect.   Superb as is the scenery, with its shadowy abysses and sunlit crags, there is awe in those black-burnt wastes, those spectral rocks, the sombre evergreen of those forests.

From the side cañons clear brooklets sing down to the hoarse and muddy river.   The heights purr with dense juniper and piñon and royal pine; the cañons whisper with cottonwoods and willows.   It is alone as death.   In nearly four thousand square miles there is not a human being.   Where once were the little corn-patches and the tall gray houses and the dimpled naked babes of thousands of the Acadians of the Southwest, the deer, the puma, the bear, and the turkey lord it again.   Even the Indians seldom visit it, and not a dozen white men have seen its wonders. Yet it contains the largest village of artificial caves in the world, the only great stone "idols" in the United States, and many another value—including the scene of one of the most remarkable stormings in military history.

When the Hero Twins had led forth man from the inner wombs of earth to light through Shi-p'a-pú, the Black Lake of Tears; and the Winter-Wizards had frozen the infinite mud so that there could be going; and the First Men had fallen out and fallen apart, a wandering band of the Quéres halted in this digitate wilderness.   Here was water, here was timber.   Above all, here was safety.   And here they sat down.   It was their own wilderness, and away from its incomparable area they have never since cared to rove. It is identified with them—with their hopes and fears, their loves and wars, and wanderings.

Their first town was in the noble cañon of the Tyú-on-yi, now also known as the Rito de los Frijoles, in

THE TYÚ-ON-YI—CACIQUE'S HOUSE.

the northern part of this plateau. Here the Quéres drew a prehistoric diagram which would have saved a vast amount of foolish theorizing, if science had earlier poked its nose out-of-doors in pursuit of fact.

The fable of the so-called Cliff-builders and Cave-dwellers, as a distinct race or races, has been absolutely exploded in science. The fact is, that the cliff-dwellers and the cave-dwellers of the Southwest were

Pueblo Indians, pure and simple. Even a careless
eye can find the proof in every corner of the Southwest. It was a question not of race, but of physical
geography. The Pueblo cut his garment according
to his cloth, and whether he burrowed his house, or
built it of mud bricks or stone-bricks or cleft stone,
atop a cliff or in caves or shelves of its face, depended
simply upon his town-site. The one inflexible rule
was security, and to gain that he took the " shortest
cut " offered by his surroundings. When he found
himself—as he sometimes did in his volcanic range—
in a region of tufa cliffs, he simply whittled out his
residence. In the commoner hard-rock cañons, he
built stone houses in whatever safest place. In the
valleys, he made and laid adobes. He sometimes
even dovetailed all these varieties of architecture in
one and the same settlement.

The Tyú-on-yi, the first known home of Cochití, is
one of the unique beauties of the Southwest. As a
cañon, it is but five or six miles long, and at the widest a quarter of a mile across. Its extreme depth
does not exceed two thousand feet. There are scores
of greater cañons in this neglected land ; but there
is only one Tyú-on-yi. At the *Bocas*, where it enters
the gorge of the Rio Grande, it is deepest, narrowest, grimmest. A few hundred yards above these
savage jaws was the town-site. A ribbon of irrigably
level land a few rods wide, threaded by a sparkling
rivulet, hemmed with glistening cliffs of white pumice-
stone fifteen hundred feet tall, murmurous with stately
pines and shivering aspens, shut on the west by the
long slope of the Jara, on the east by the pinching of
its own giant walls—that is the Tyú-on-yi. That,

but more. For along the sheer and noble northern
cliff crumble the bones of a human past—a past of
heroism and suffering and romance. In the foot of
that stone snow-bank new shadows play hide and
seek in strange old hollows, that were not gnawed by
wind and rain, but by as patient man. It is an enchanted valley. The spell of the Southwest is upon
it. The sun's white benediction, the hush of Nature's
heart, the invisible haunting of a *Once*—that utmost
of all solitudes, the silence that *was* life—they wrap
it in an atmosphere almost unique. It is an impression of a lifetime. The great cave-villages of the
Pu-yé and the Shú-fin-né, in their white castle-buttes
thirty miles up the river, are not to be compared with
it, though they are its nearest parallel in the world.
It is not only a much larger village than either of
them, but with a beauty and charm altogether peerless.

It was a large town for the prehistoric United
States—a town of fifteen hundred to two thousand
souls. The latter figure was never exceeded by *any*
aboriginal "city" of the Southwest. The line of artificial cave-rooms is a couple of miles long, and in tiers
of one, two, and three stories. With their "knives"
of chipped volcanic glass for sole tools, the Cochiteños builded their matchless village. First, they
hewed in the face of the cliff their inner rooms.
These were generally rectangular, about six by eight,
with arched roofs ; but sometimes large, and sometimes circular. Some were sole houses and had tiny
outer doorways in the rock and as tiny ones from
room to room within—a plan which has given rise,
in ruins oftener seen by the theorizer, to the fable of

THE TYÚ-ON-YI—WALLED CAVE-ROOMS.

cliff-dwelling pigmies. The builders, in fact, were of
present Pueblo stature, and made these wee doorways
simply for security. The man of the house could af-

ford time to enter edgewise on hands and knees ; an
enemy could not. Some rooms combine cave and
masonry, having an artificial outer wall. And some,
again, were merely cave-storehouses and retreats
back of a stone-brick house. Outside, against the
foot of the cliffs, is the chaos of fallen masonry. The
builders adopted a plan peculiar to this plateau. With
their same flakes of obsidian they sawed the tufa into
large and rather regular bricks, and of these exclusively laid their masonry in an excellent mortar of
adobe. A restoration of the Tyú-on-yi would show a
long line of three-story terraced houses of these tufa-
blocks against the foot of that weird cliff ; the rafters
inserted into still visible mortises in its face ; without
doors or windows in the ground floor, and abristle
with the spar-like ladders by which the upper stories
were reached, and, back through their rooms, the
caves. None of the outer houses are now standing—
the best of their walls are but four or five feet high—
but the dim procession of centuries that has toppled
them to ruin has dealt kindlier with the caves. The
caked smoke of the hearth still clings—half fossil—on
the low-arched roofs and around the tiny window
smoke-holes. The very plastering of the walls—for
the home had already reached such painstaking that
even the smooth rock must be hidden by a film of
cement—is generally intact. The little niches, where
trinkets were laid, are there ; and in one house is
even the stone frame of the prehistoric handmill. In
several places are cave-rooms with their fronts and
partitions of tufa masonry still entire ; and one lovely
little nook, well up the cañon, has still a perfect house
unlike any other prehistoric building in America—

walled cave, wood-framed door and windows, and all.
In this climate wood is almost eternal.   Timbers that
have been fully exposed since 1670 in the " Gran
Quivíra " have not even lost their ornamental carv-

THE TYÚ-ON-YI—SECOND- AND THIRD- STORY CAVES ; AND MORTISES FOR
RAFTERS OF THE OUTER HOUSES.

ings, and beams of vastly greater age are still sound.
Here and there down the slope, toward the brook, are
the remains of the circular subterranean estufas wherein the male village dwelt ; and in a strangely scalloped
swell of the cliff is still the house of the Cacique—a
very fair hemisphere of a room, cut from the rock,

with a floor diameter of some fifteen feet. Not far away, beside the rivulet, are the ruins of a huge communal house—one of the so-called "round" ruins. Exploration always shows that these alleged circles are merely irregular polygons. There never was a round pueblo; though the estufas were very generally round and there were other small single buildings of the same shape. The usual stone artifects are rarely to be found here, for roving Navajos have assiduously stripped the place of everything of aboriginal use. Only now and then a rude obsidian knife, an arrow-point, or a battered stone axe rewards the relic-seeker—beyond the innumerable fragments of ancient pottery.

So exceptionally complete are the links in a story which may very well go far back of William the Conqueror, that we even have legendary hints of the subdivisions of this immemorial village; and in a cave-room of the cluster which has suffered most from the erosion of the cliff, I once stumbled upon gentle José Hilario Montoya, the now Governor of the new Cochití, wrapped in his blanket and in reverie. He had stolen away from us, to dream an hour in the specific house that was of his own first grandfathers.

We have no means of knowing just how long the strange white town of the Rito has been deserted, but it has been many, many centuries; for its hunted people built successive towns, and farmed and fought and had a history in each of six later homes before the written history of America began. Though eternally harassed by the Navajos, the Tyú-on-yi held its own, we are told, until destroyed by its own brethren. The conditions of life there (and in all

prehistoric pueblos) and the interwarring of the various tribes are drawn with photographic accuracy of

JOSÉ HILARIO MONTOYA, GOVERNOR PUEBLO OF COCHITÍ.

detail in that little-read but archæologically precious
novel, " The Delight-Makers."

The survivors of the final catastrophe abandoned
their ruined town in the Rito, and moving a day's
march to the south, established themselves upon the
table-top of the great Potrero de las Vacas. They

were now seven or eight miles west of the chasm of
the Rio Grande, and on the summit of the tongue-
plateau between two of its principal side-cañons.
They were a mile from water—the sparkling brooklet
which flows past the Cueva Pintada—and therefore
from their farms. But feeling this inconvenience little so long as it gave safety, they reared among the
contorted junipers a new town—essentially unlike the
quaint combination-pueblo of the Rito, but like to a
more common pattern. It was the typical rectangular stone box of continuous houses, all facing in.
Here on the grim mesa, amid a wilderness of appalling solitude, they worried out the tufa blocks, and
builded their fortress-city, and fended off the prowling Navajo, and fought to water and home again,
and slept with an arrow on the string. How many
generations of bronze babies frolicked in this lap of
danger ; and rose to arrowy youth that loved between sieges ; and to gray-heads that watched and
counselled ; and to still clay that cuddled to the long
sleep in rooms thenceforth sealed forever, there is no
reckoning—nor when was the red foray, whereof
their legends tell, of an unknown tribe which finished
the town of the Mesa of the Cows. But when the
decimated Quéres left that noble site, they left, beside
their fallen home, a monument of surpassing interest.
The Nahuatl culture, which filled Mexico with huge
and hideous statues chiselled from the hardest rock,
was never paralleled within the United States ; for
our aborigines had no metal tools whatever until after
the Conquest. New Mexican work in stone (aside
from the making of implements and beads) was confined to tiny fetiches which were rather *worn* than

carved to shape, and to a few larger but very crude fetiches of softer rock. The only examples of life-size carvings, or of any *alto relievo*, ever found in the enormous range of the Pueblos, are the four astonishing figures which were, and are, the homotypes of the chase-gods of wandering Cochití.

A few hundred yards up the dim trail which leads from the ruined town of the Potrero de las Vacas toward the near peaks, one comes suddenly upon a strange aboriginal Stonehenge. Among the tattered piñons and sprawling cedars is a lonely enclosure fenced with great slabs of tufa set up edgewise. This enclosure, which is about thirty feet in diameter, has somewhat of the shape of a tadpole; for at the south-east end its oval tapers into an alley five feet wide and twenty long, similarly walled. In the midst of this unique roofless temple of the Southwestern Druids are the weathered images of two cougars, carved in high relief from the bedrock of the mesa. The figures are life-size; and even the erosion of so many centuries has not gnawed them out of recognition. The heads are nearly indistinguishable, and the fore-shoulders have suffered; but the rest of the sculpture, to the very tips of the outstretched tails, is perfectly clear. The very attitude of the American lion is preserved—the flat, stealthy, compact crouch that precedes the mortal leap. Artistically, of course, the statues are crude; but zoologically, they bear the usual Indian truthfulness. As to their transcendent archæologic value and great antiquity, there can be no question. The circumstantial evidence is conclusive that they were carved by the Cochiteños during the life of the town of the Potrero de las Vacas.

The cougar, puma, or "mountain-lion"—mo-keit-cha, in the Quéres tongue—is to the Pueblo the head of animate creation. In this curious mythology, each of the six like groups of divinities, "the Trues," which dwell respectively at the six cardinal points, includes a group of deified dumb animals. They are Trues also, and are as carefully ranked as the higher spirits, or even more definitely. The beasts of prey, of course, stand highest; and of them, and of all animals, the puma is Ka-béy-de, commander-in-chief. Under him there are minor officials; the buffalo is captain of the ruminants; the eagle, of birds; the crotalus, of reptiles. There are even several other animal gods of the hunt—the bear, the wolf, the coyote—but he is easily supreme. The hunter carries a tiny stone image of this most potent patron, and invokes it with strange incantations at every turn of the chase. But it was reserved for the Cochiteños to invent and realize a life-size fetich—therefore, one nearer the actual divinity symbolized, and more powerful. And from that far, forgotten day to this incongruous one, the stone lions of Cochití have never lost their potency. Worshipped continually for longer ages than Saxon history can call its own, they are worshipped still. No important hunt would even now be undertaken by the trustful folk of Cochití without first repairing to the stone pumas, to anoint their stolid heads with face-paint and the sacred meal, and to breathe their breath of power.

But now the town of the lions had fallen, and a second migration was imperative. In this new move to checkmate the tireless aggressor, the Cochiteños took a sort of "knight's leap." They dropped fifteen

hundred feet from the mesa's top to the cañon, and
thence at a right angle three miles down the brook,
namely, to the Cueva Pintada. The site of this, their
third known town, which they called Tsé-ki-a-tán-yi,
was far ahead in safety and in picturesqueness of the
second. In both these qualities it somewhat recalls
the peerless Rito. The cañon is wider and not so
deep, but of similar formation, and similarly wooded
and watered. As always, the wanderers chose its
noblest point. There the northern cliff of white
pumice is five hundred feet high, and in its face is a
great natural cave like a basin set on edge, fifty feet
above the ground. Along the foot of this fine cliff
they hewed out their cave-rooms and built their tufa
masonry, and in the arch of the great natural cave itself they hollowed other chambers, attainable only by
dizzy toeholes in the sheer rock. The Painted Cave
seems to have had some of the uses of a shrine, and
along the crescent of its inner wall may still be traced
prehistoric pictographs (along with more modern
ones) done in the red ochre which abounds farther
up the cañon. There are figures of the Kö-sha-re,
the delight-makers, and of the sacred snake whose
cult—once universal among the Pueblos—has still
such astounding survival at Moqui ; and of the round,
bright house of the Sun-Father and of the morning
and evening stars, and many other precious symbols.

At last the turn of Tsé-ki-a-tán-yi came too, and
there was a day when they who had burrowed in its
gray cliffs must bid it farewell. The cause of this migration is not certain. It may have been moral or
military ; omen of divine displeasure, or merely an
overdose of Navajo—for the whole region was cease-

lessly harried by this most powerful race of desert
pirates. At all events, the beset Quéres had finally
to abandon their third town and seek a fourth. This
time they moved south a short march and built Rǎ-
tya, whose ruins are now known as San Miguel.
Here again they dwelt and suffered and made history;
and from here again they were at last compelled, by
supernatural or hostile pressure, to move on. Their
fifth stone town they built in the Cañada de Cochití,
twelve miles northwest from the present pueblo, and
named it Cuá-pa. There was, and is, a lovely thread
of a valley, just widening from the dark jaws of the
cañon which splits the Potrero Viejo from its giant
brother to the north.

Half-way back on the trail to the Cueva, atop the
almost inaccessible Potrero de los Idolos, Bandelier—
who was also the discoverer of the Rito, the Cueva
Pintada, and the Potrero de las Vacas with its wonderful images—found two other stone cougars. They
are life-size, but of different design from those of the
northern *potrero;* less weathered, and evidently of
later, though still prehistoric, origin. They, also,
were carved in high relief from the bedrock with obsidian knives; they, likewise, faced south and were
surrounded by a fence of tufa slabs. But they have
not been as undisturbed. When I was there, I had
been preceded by that unknown genius against whose
invasion no shrine is sacred—the vandal whom it were
libel to call a brute and flattery to dub a fool. Finding these gray old images crouching on and of the
monumental rock—a rock larger than any three
buildings in America—his meteoric intellect at once
conceived that there must be treasure under them—

" Montezuma's treasure," of course. And forthwith
he drilled beside them, and applied giant powder, and
blew up twenty feet ; and then gophered a tunnel below.   It is to be regretted that his bones were not

THE CUEVA PINTADA.

left in his mine.   The explosion shattered one of the
lions to fragments ; but the other, providentially, was
lifted up with a slab of its base, and lies uninjured at
one side of the hole.   Though life-size, it is not so
long as its brethren above the Cueva Pintada, since
the tail is curled up along the spine.   Nor does it

seem to have been quite so well done—that is, it is a
trifle more conventionalized. But it is equally unmis-
takable, not merely to the archæologist, but even to
anyone who has ever seen the greatest cat of the Western Hemisphere. There has been a proposition by
someone to cut these lions free from the mother-rock
and transport them to Washington. Of course, the
fact that their archæologic value would be gone if
they were thus shorn of their surroundings, was lost
sight of; as was the further fact that they are the
property of citizens of the United States. The Cochiteños would resist the removal with their last drop of
blood; and in such a cause they shall not be without
allies. Plaster models would give all that science
needs, or has legal or moral right to take.

Driven in time from the Cañada, as they had been
driven from four previous towns, the Quéres climbed
the seven-hundred-foot cliffs of the Potrero Viejo,
which overhangs the Cañada. Here was their sixth
town—Há-nut Cochití, or Cochití Above—and their
most impregnable. Nowhere save by the three vertiginous trails is it possible to scale that aërial fortress; and we may presume that here at last they
were able to defy their savage neighbors. With time,
however, the difficulties of farming and watering at
such long range seem to have induced them to remove to the banks of the Rio Grande, just where it
emerges from its grewsome gorge to the widening
vales of Peña Blanca. Here they raised their seventh
pueblo, this time largely of adobe; and here they
were when the history of America began. There is
nothing to indicate that the Cochití which has been
known now for three hundred and fifty years, has

been longer occupied than was any one of the six
towns which preceded it; though of course the presumption is that it has. Here the Spanish world-
openers found the town, and here the Cochiteños
voluntarily became vassals of Spain and were baptized into the church of the new God. Here, too,
nearly a century and a half later, they helped to
brew that deadliest insurrection which ever broke on
United States soil; and on that red August 10, 1680,
their warriors were of the swarthy avalanche that befell the undreaming Spaniards. They had a hand in
the slaying of the three priests of their parish, who
were stationed at Santo Domingo; and were among
the leading spirits of all those bloody years of the
Pueblo rebellion. The only fight in which they are
known to have figured largely, however, was at the
reconquest. When Diego de Vargas, the *Recon-
quistador*, came, they abandoned Cochití and went
back to their long-ruined citadel on the Potrero Viejo. This seventh town-moving did not save them;
for in the spring of 1694 Vargas and his "army" of
one hundred and fifty men stormed that aboriginal
Gibraltar. In the desperate but short assault only
twenty-one Indians were slain. Indeed, the decima-
tion of the Cochiteños was due not at all to the Spaniards, but to their one-sided wars with the Navajos
and with other Pueblos; to epidemics, and to social
centrifuge—for the legendary hints are strong that
not only Cochití but *all* the Quéres pueblos originated in the Tyú-on-yi. If this be true, the six present
Quéres pueblos to the south and west of Cochití,
with their prehistoric predecessors—for each had its
town-movings—were doubtless founded by early

rovers from the Rito, until all were gone from the first nest save the later wanderers whom we have been following.

After the reconquest the Cochiteños abandoned

THE OLDEST OF THE QUÉRES.

their second town on the Potrero Viejo, and moving for the eighth time, returned to their present pueblo, where they have ever since remained. It is seldom

that any of them visit the old homes.   Only when
there is to be a ceremonial hunt do they trudge away
to their ancient Chase-Fetiches to drink the mighty
breath of Mokeitcha.   The trails are so fearfully
rough that one can go all the way to the Rito much
sooner afoot than on even the tireless Indian pony ;
and they are lonely now, and grown very dim.   The
ankle-deep wee crystals of the potrero-tops outsparkle
the Valley of the Rocs, unscuffled by passing feet.
The wild turkey drinks unscared from the Rito de los
Frijoles, and blinks at its sun-bewildered walls.   The
tawny puma purrs in the white light beside his gray
stone prototypes on the Potrero de las Vacas or the
Potrero de los Idolos.   And Cochití, at rest at last,
dreams on its sunward gravel bank along the swirl-
ing Rio Grande, and tills its happy fields, and goes to
its Christian mass, and dances unto the Trues, and
forgets that ever there was war and wandering.

VII

THE APACHE WARRIOR

THE APACHE WARRIOR

THERE is no manner of doubt that Leonidas and his three hundred were very worthy citizens; but it is evident that they missed their vocation. Their military intentions were creditable but crude, and lacked scientific light. Of the twofold functions of the ideal warrior they knew but one side—to do the utmost possible damage to the enemy. But in the twin duty they failed utterly—and after the general fashion of civilized warfare. War seems to be the one thing which civilization makes impossible of scientific treatment. We have to play it checker-fashion, or on Mosaic principles, buying an eye with an eye, giving a tooth for a tooth. We frill the general clumsiness with alleged strategy; but Providence remains on the side of the heaviest battalions. Our own great war was solved on that principle. As long as the military geniuses prevailed, we were very near to be whipped. But then came along a tanner with a tanner's business head, and began counting. He summed up that the North had the most men; and when he came to that conclusion the Rebellion was doomed. He could afford to be beaten in every battle, to lose man for man, or two for one; and when the game was ended, he would have men left. It was on that line that the civil checker-game was played and won.

But the *art* of war is realized in another way. The object is to kill without being killed; to conquer and still live to enjoy the fruits of victory. The brute courage which dies fighting is often useful, sometimes admirable; but it is not the highest quality. The bull-dog is the only canine so brutally ignorant as to hold one grip till death. The higher dogs know better—they snap and dodge. Brains were made to save the hide as well as shoe-leather. If Leonidas had been an Apache, he would have killed off the Persian myriads a handful at a time, without once being seen by them. Three hundred Spartan wives and mothers would each have been a husband or a son ahead by the transaction; and we should have lost one of the most brilliant examples wherewith we are wont to call heroism.

For certain reasons, which would be tedious of discussion here, the ideal war-maker is found in the savage, who has learned just enough from civilization to avoid its military follies—which are simply an enlargement of what he practised before his graduation. Uncelebrated in song, unappreciated by history—and thereby docked of his due proportion on Fame's canvas—there is one tawny figure to a brief inspection of whom I would invite you.

For centuries which no pen has recorded, the Apache has been the most notable and the least noted of warriors. He has been the scourge of a territory greater than Europe, minus Russia. To this day his name is a bugbear throughout an area in which New England could be irrecoverably lost. It is not numbers that gave him his reputation. At the outside, his people cannot muster six thousand. Of his twenty tribes, seventeen no longer contain so much as the seeds of war. More than a decade ago they were brought into eternal submission by that silent, large-hearted, broad-minded, belied but unanswering soldier, George Crook. The Apache who remained the ideal warrior was the Chiricahua, so called by the gentlemen who have clinched their careless blunders in our literature. His real name is Chihuicahui, after his rocky fastnesses "the Turkey Mountain." The last virile remnant of a shattered race, it long looked uncertain if he ever would be whipped—crushed, he never was. He was steered into the channels of quasi-civilization less by his defeats than by his insight. In 1886 three hundred and fifty-five of him were quietly farming upon the White Mountain Reservation, Arizona; seventy-seven were lying in a Florida prison, and thirty-four were laughing to scorn the power of a nation of sixty millions. That is, the sober majority had accepted the inevitable quietly and with a growing content, in which they will remain so long as a half-honorable policy is maintained toward them. The desperadoes were untamable, and yielded at last, not because they were beaten, but because they got their own terms.

On May 17, 1885, thirty-four Chihuicahui men, eight well-grown boys, and ninety-two women and children exchanged the reservation for the warpath. Among them were Geronimo, Mangus, Chihuahua, and other aboriginal Marions. Up to April 1, 1886, these thirty-four encumbered warriors had killed between three and four hundred people in

the United States and Mexico; and despite the un-
tiring pursuit of the most experienced and most successful Indian-fighter our army has ever had, lost but

THE APACHE WARRIOR, VICTORIO.

two of their own number, killed. A dozen of their
women and children were captured after a campaign
whose activity and hardships no civilized war could
parallel ; and a mixed threescore at last came in of

their own free will to rest from their travels. After that, for six months, the remaining twenty warriors, hampered by fourteen women, baffled the fairly frantic pursuit of two thousand soldiers, pushed by an able general, not to mention several thousand Mexican soldiers. They killed something less than a hundred people, kept Sonora, Chihuahua, Arizona, and New Mexico on the tip-toe of terror, and never lost a man. That is the sort of warrior the Apache was.

Physically, the Chihuicahui became the flower of his people. It is not presumable that he had any initial advantage over his cousins, the Tontos, the Hualapais, the Jicarillas, and other Apaches. That he is now far superior to them can be due only to his longer scholarship in the curriculum of the warpath. As a rule, he is not of imposing height, though Mangus Colorado, a great chief in several ways, stood six feet and a half tall. The Chihuicahui majority, however, are of medium stature, straight (without the stiffness which generally twins with the American attempt to be erect), compact, and strongly built, but seldom heavy; and always of that easy carriage which belongs alone to perfect physical condition. There is never the classic protuberance of knotted muscle so affected by our athletes; nor are they in fact so powerful in foot-pounds as highly developed Caucasians. Their arms and legs are smooth and round; rarely scrawny and rarely fat. A grand breadth and depth of chest and generous substantiality of back are observable in all.

The Chihuicahui head is fairly well moulded and of good size. The straight black hair is generally trimmed at the level of the shoulder-blades. The

11

features are strongly and rather sharply marked; the aquiline nose not generally heavy, nor the lips over full. The eyes are sparkful, restless, and unfathomable. The face is never blank, yet never legible. It seems as if the nerves and muscles by which, in civilization, the brain reflects its images upon the countenance, had all been cut. There is not a twitch, a shade, a change by which the keenest of us may read what is behind. And meantime, through this impassive mask, your tawny *vis-à-vis*—a reader who never opened a book save the great volume of nature—is searching your very soul with indifferent eyes which never look at you. He can come very near telling what you had for breakfast. He has kept the senses which nature gave man, and has educated them as few of us are ever educated in anything. No sound is so faint, no trace so delicate, as to escape his notice; nor, noticed, as to elude his comprehension. A pebble with its earthward side turned up, a broken marguerite, the invisible flash of a gun-barrel ten miles away—he notes and understands them all. He will stoop to a trail so dim that the best Caucasian observer would not dream of its presence, and tell correctly how long ago that imprint was made. The arid hill-side or the dusty maze of the highway are an open book to him, with full detail of when and how many passed, Indians or whites, men or women, by night or day. With the practice of a lifetime the best Saxon scout does not attain a comparable acuteness.

The secret of the Chihuicahui warrior is chiefly his physical training. The white athlete begins, at best, his training at eighteen. He thinks himself, and is thought, a prodigy of faithfulness if he gives six hours a day to exercise. He is out-of-doors, at the limit, one-third of the time. He eats heartily, in a house ; sleeps heavily, in a house—*lives* between walls. His regimen bulges each muscle to a clear-cut, knotted cord ; it develops enormous strength but not supreme stay. Endurance is the child of such hardships as he does not care to face.

The Chihuicahui is born out-of-doors ; and until his comrades pile above his clay the rocks which shall cheat the prowling coyote, he draws no breath elsewhere. He comes to a heritage of athletic centuries. The very mother who bore him is a sturdy animal capable of tiring out the flower of the white usurpers. He is always learning from nature at first hands ; and his livelihood and life depend upon his observant receptivity.

To the natural acuteness of all his kind, the country of his nativity adds a finish peculiarly his own. The Indian-ness of an Indian—his keenness, courage, and cunning—seem to be in the inverse ratio of his larder. In the easy, grassy, well-watered, game-populous regions, the aborigine was comparatively a lazy, fat-bodied, and fat-witted brute. In the grim deserts of the Southwest he became the most tireless, acute, and terrible man. His whole existence a hardship, a struggle with a nature from whose gaunt fist only the most persistent and skilful wrenching can wring bare life, the Apache was whetted to a ferocity of edge, an endurance of temper, which were impossible in a more endurable country. He earned the eye of the kite, the ear of the cat, the cunning of the fox, the ferocious courage and tirelessness of the gray wolf. Over the crags of his arid ranges he could travel farther in a day than the world's champion on a cinder track, and keep it up for more days. When the outbreak of May, 1885, occurred, the renegades —of whom ninety per cent. were women and children —never drew rein to eat, drink, or rest until they were one hundred and twenty miles from the reservation. The officers and men selected by Crook to pursue that band into Mexico were all picked athletes—sunburnt young fellows with muscles of steel. For ten hours before they reached the spot where the gallant Crawford was assassinated by Mexican banditti, every white man in the company was crutched on either side by an Apache scout, who dragged him along by the arm. At the time of the fight they had been marching for forty hours without food or fire. The six Caucasians were nearly dead with exertion ; the seventy-nine Apache scouts, who had travelled much farther in the same time, were fresh. In a word, the Apache could wear out in physical endurance the most enduring of his white foes. Hunger he could stand twice as long, and thirst four times as long, as the best of them.

No less important to his success than this great endurance, was his method of war—and that is a recent factor. Up to fifteen years ago the Apache fought like a cinnamon bear, or a Saxon, knowing no better. He " stood up to it," and was fearfully punished. With mesquite-bow and quartz-tipped arrows —and maybe an occasional musket in the tribe—he waged plucky but hopeless battle against our disciplined and well-armed troops. But, conservative as he is of the old traditions, it did not take him long to see that give-and-take did not pay. After his Waterloo in 1874, by Crook, his policy out-fabianed Fabius. It was the policy of invisibility. Throughout the two last campaigns it was a problem not of fighting but of finding him. He has ravaged Arizona for a month along a zigzag line of march of a thousand miles, with every soldier in the department in hot chase; and never so much as once seen by his pursuers. But they have felt him. Spurred to fresh haste by the hideous scenes about some smoking ruin of a lonely cabin, the soldiers press angrily along the fresh trail, across the arid plain, up the still cañon. *Pyang! Pyang!* From behind yon prickly rosette of the aloe, yon bowlder, yon tuft of bear-grass, sickly little curls of smoke; and for each faint spiral a soldier has tumbled. It is no place to stop and fight—as well put your head under a trip-hammer. The only thing to be done is to get out of that death-trap; and those who are left get out. By the time they are ready to continue the pursuit, the pursued are ten miles away.

Were he a civilized soldier, the Apache's policy of elusiveness would avail him little; but he is not. Civilization sacrifices the individual to the aggregate. Until personality is submerged more or less, there can be no community. But the Apache has not been socially drowned. He is the essence of individuality; and particularly in war. He is the military Louis XIV., and can say with fuller pertinence: "The army is I." He is commander-in-chief, division-commander, brigade-commander, colonel, major, captain, rank and file, signal corps, engineers, commissary, and transportation. He is always a warrior and never a soldier. The soldier is a machine which moves only when the lever is pulled.   It steps, turns, whistles, expectorates, by word of command.   It is, like most of the other necessary lessons of civilization a life-training against self-reliance.   As a matter of fact our troops had to be desoldierized as completely as possible before they were of any earthly use in a campaign against Indians who had turned war into a science.   The Apache, after that, had nothing to un-learn.   He was self-reliant, self-contained, and self-sufficing.   He needed nothing which the Saxon had to have—from food to a leader.   He was equal by himself to every emergency of the desert and of battle.

With his perfect physique, he had a military adapt-ability absolutely elastic.   When our troops started on a campaign of months in the desert, they must take supplies to last.   The saddle and pack animals could not be worked to death in a week, but must be kept efficient to the end of the campaign.   Here the Apache had a material though adventitious superi-ority.   He started astride his best horse, and rode it at top speed until it fell.   Timely, before this junct-ure, he had raided some rancho, and gathered fresh stock.   He put his knife to the throat of his fallen steed, and leaped upon a fresh one, whose fate was to be as soon and as certain.   Little wonder, then, if, with his own greater endurance, he travelled incredi-ble distances as compared with those who could not afford to kill a horse or two a day.   For instance, Ulzana and his raiders were on our soil about seven weeks in the fall of 1885.   They killed thirty-eight soldiers, citizens, and friendly Indians, lost but one of their own number, and were never caught sight of by the troops or civilians in pursuit. In that enormous ride they used up twenty mounts apiece—two hundred and sixty horses. How did they get hold of so many? A couple of examples will show.

While the lamented Crawford was hanging like a gray wolf to the trail of Ulzana's band, they took refuge in their own Chihuicahui mountains. Hard pressed there, they made a night dash to the westward, across the broad Sulphur Springs Valley. Their stock was on its last legs; and while the rest of the band pounded ahead, three lone bucks descended upon the sulphur springs ranch-house. Inside the strong building snored a dozen cowboys, their six-shooters under the hay pillows, their Winchesters beside them. Their animals were in a corral of stout palisade, with gates locked and barred. The three invaders borrowed a hatchet from the wood-pile, chopped down enough palisades to open a gap, took all the horses, and rode away.

Crawford kept up the chase. The remounted renegades swept through the Dragoon and Mule Mountains; and then, whipping square to the left, made again for the Chihuicahui range. The day after they reached them, Crawford came to the spot where they had stabbed to death every one of their horses and taken to cover like a bunch of quail. Then he thought he had them. At this time the cattlemen of the San Simon Valley (just east of the range) were assembled for their fall round-up, and had camped in force at a rancho in the mouth of White-tail Cañon. They knew the hostiles were near, but were confident in numbers. In the morning, when they awoke and rubbed their secure eyes, every last pony was

gone, reata and all. The raiders had " scooped "
thirty of the best horses in Arizona; and Crawford's
tremendous pursuit found only the trail of these fresh
steeds sweeping far down into Sonora, where the
savage riders were secure.

An expedition against the hostiles was perforce
accompanied by a pack-train of twenty to one hundred and fifty patient mules—the only transport available in that rugged land. The pack-train carried rations for the probable length of the campaign. It
carried also water, ammunition, and cooking uten-
sils. Long cut off from this slow-moving base, the
command would perish in such a wilderness. But
the Apache had, and needed, no pack-train. His ammunition was stored in numerous belts about his
body. His commissary was the unit of simplicity.
There were no pots, no frying-pans, no canned goods,
no cases of " hard-tack and salt horse." When he
moved at leisure he carried a load of jerked meat,
roasted mescal, and other desert dainties; but these
were discarded without hesitation in time of need. A
white man would have starved to death without his
commissary; but the Apache had an elastic adapta-
bility which enabled him to eat more, or live on less,
as circumstances might require, than anyone else.
To him the desert afforded a menu when he had time
to stop for it. He strolls over to yonder greasewood
bush, wherein is a dry tangle of leaves and twigs,
looking like a bit of lodged drift. With imperative
cudgel he punches, belabors, and scatters this litter,
and presently extracts a score of fat prairie-mice—a
feast indeed. Or, with a long and supple switch he
trudges among the sand hillocks with intermittent

lashings of the ground, and returns with a toothsome string of gracile lizards. Hapless the rattlesnake who shall erect himself on burring coil to make mouths at an Apache when the belt hangs loose ! Evicted from that lozenged hide, his delicate gray meat shall make a dainty *entrée*. All these are seasonable meats to the Apache when hunger is to be put to sleep ; but they are not his only resources thereunto. His plan of campaign combines commissary and transportation with supreme neatness. When his hardy bronco at last succumbs to hardships which would break down a locomotive, his services are not yet ended. The tenderest portions of him—if tenderness at all can be predicted of those leathery tissues—are hastily hacked off to dangle in sun-cured strips across the back of his successor. His long intestine, mayhap, is cleaned —after Chihuicahui notions of cleaning—and becomes a water-keg of great capacity and matchless portability. If transportation is adequate, twenty feet or so of this unique canteen is wound around a led-horse ; if horses be scarce, four or five feet of it is slung, life-preserver fashion, about the neck of some athletic brave, and gives a family water for a week.

The hostile does not wholly subsist, however, upon meat and water. Bread is disregarded on the war-path, for flour would be too difficult of transportation. But again he lays nature under contribution, and with wonted success. It is surprising how the limited flora of his sterile range caters to his every want. Nearly every plant plays into his hand some trump card of utility. Chief of all is that paradoxical growth the mescal, an aloe whose repellent daggers ambush almost infinite generosity. Shut an Apache

up with it alone, and it gives him a livelihood. With·
out it, the Apache question would not have taken one-
half so long to settle.   This bristling benefactor gives
the aborigine a quasi-bread which is at once nutritious
and lasting ; two athletic intoxicants ; thread, and
even clothing, and countless minor staples.   It grows
throughout the whole vast realm the Apache ranged,
an ever-present base of supplies.   When the raiders
had gained enough on their pursuers to afford a few
days' rest, a mescal-roast was in order.   A pit was
dug, and a fire of the greasewood's crackling roots
kept up therein until the surroundings were well
heated.   Upon the hot stones of the pit was laid a
layer of the pulpiest sections of the mescal; upon this
a layer of wet grass ; then another layer of mescal,
and another of grass, and so on.   Finally, the whole
pile was tightly banked over with earth, and nature
left to take her course.   The roasting—or, rather,
steaming—takes from two to four days.   And how
does the untutored *chef* know when his desert clam-
bake is done ?   By a very simple process.   When he
banks the pile with earth, he arranges a few · long
bayonets of the mescal so that their tips shall project.
When it seems to him that the roast should be done,
he withdraws one of these plugs.   If the lower end is
well-done he uncovers the heap and proceeds to feast ;
if still too rare, he covers the hole and possesses his
soul in patience until a later experiment proves the
baking.   The roasted mescal suggests, in looks and
taste, a mixture of molasses candy and jute threads.
It does not upon first acquaintance endear itself to
the American palate, but soon effects a reconciliation.
It is very nutritious, and can be kept six months.

Another valuable food staple is the bean of the thorny and unpromising mesquite. Reduced to meal, it makes palatable cakes. The fruit of the Spanish bayonet, dried in the sun, makes a fair lunch, suggesting dates. Even the mountain acorns furnish excellent meal. This by no means exhausts the Apache's bill of fare ; but it suffices to show how he keeps well nourished in a country whose visible means of support are of vagrant slimness. The White Mountain reservation, the Apache's lawful home, and the vast range of the Sierra Madre (Mexico), his favorite unlawful refuge, are full of game—particularly deer, turkey, and fish. Add to this the sheep and cattle of a thousand ranchos, and it may be seen that after living robustly on the desert, the hostile can live luxuriously at certain oases.

Not less radical than the Apache's change of policy within a generation, has been his change of armament. From the bow-and-arrow he has graduated to skilled use of the best modern facilities for murder. He became, in his last campaigns, better equipped than his official pursuers. He had the best makes of rifles, and carried the finest field-glasses in Arizona. His sixshooters were of the best, and frequently had ivory handles. A couple of hundred rounds of the finest reloading cartridges were handily bestowed about him in regulation belts ; and in every mountain fastness he had *cachéd* ammunition and spare guns in plenty. Whence ? Well, money will buy anything in Arizona or Mexico. The Apache warrior always has money ; and he can always buy a gun in Tucson, not to say in the hundreds of hamlets below the line. He can do it now in time of peace ; and he could do it equally well when he was splotching half Arizona with blood.

So admirably armed, the Chihuicahui knew how to use his weapons. He might not have won so many marksmanship medals shooting across measured ground at fixed targets; but he had a way of shooting up-hill, down-hill, across plain, ravine, or ridge, and hitting what he aimed at. His marvellous eyesight, too, enables him to draw bead upon a foe who would be invisible to us. With moving targets he is at home, as when Kiowtennay, the most valued of the friendly scouts, started a peccary on the march to Cañon de los Embudos. Kiowtennay put spurs to his horse, and at full gallop sent a Winchester ball square through the brain of the galloping wild pig.

In actual battle the Apache showed the new science of Indian warfare at its best, and its superiority over our clumsy tactics. To his strategic mind the exposed charge, the holding of a hot position, seemed simply silly and unworthy of intelligent warriors. He took care that, whether advancing, retreating, or holding his ground, no inch of his tawny hide should be exposed. Only his gleaming eye was bared to hostile bullets; and that is a mark which few white riflemen can see—much less score upon—at a hundred yards. But the Apache will note the eye of a foe at even greater distance, and will stand a very fair chance of putting it out, too. The soldier found him thus entrenched among the rocks, and in reaching him was largely exposed. He could not take advantage of the ground as could his wily foe; and the consequence was that for every Apache killed in war ten or twenty of our soldiers bit the dust.

The Apache code of military ethics was more logical than handsome. He carried out in cold blood our aphorisms: "All's fair in love and war;" and "To the victors belong the spoils." He was, in fact, the most atrocious freebooter and butcher we have ever encountered. I neither apologize for nor wonder at him. He is merely what our ancestors were a millennium ago—only much abler. His war-path etiquette holds it perfectly *au fait* to kill men, women, and children; to torture, toast, and eviscerate; to burn, ravish, and rob. He himself has been robbed by the dollar, by the acre, and by the hundred miles square. When it comes to a fight, he has noticed that his own women and children are first to be killed; that their scalps are worth as much bounty in the frontier markets of the Superior Race as are the scalps of braves; and that all his personal belongings are objects of eternal solicitude to a large class of his civilized neighbors. He has not to tax his memory by many years to recall when a force of Arizona citizens marched to his reservation to butcher the aged, the women, and the babes—taking good care to call when the warriors were not at home. Those who can read recall numerous editorials, in not the smallest papers of the land, condoning that sort of extermination. Little wonder if the Apache learned the logic of his Christian foes, and retorted with equal force. By the way, however, he is libelled in one immaterial point. The Apache is not a scalper. Nor is the Navajo. Scalping is essentially a custom of the Indians of the plains and forests, the northern and eastern tribes. There have been cases known in which the Apache took a scalp, and many of him have been scalped by Saxons; but the one is as alien to national customs as the other. In a majority of cases, he merely kills—unless the foe is the object of an old grudge, or something of the sort. In that event the victor tries to get even by an infinite hideousness and complexity of mutilation.

In speaking of the causes which made the Apache pre-eminent among warriors, I have reserved to the last one of the most important—his country. Perhaps there is no more fearful campaigning-ground in the world.

The original realm which this Bedouin of the New World terrorized for centuries, was of enormous size. From the Arkansaw River in Colorado to Durango, Mexico; and from San Antonio, Texas, to where the Colorado laps the arid hem of California's eden, he was felt. Ten years ago, decimated and restricted as he had been, his outbreaks carried terror over the majority of this huge area; his boundaries being a little narrowed upon the north and east. The difficulty of cornering a dozen or fifty supremely elusive foes in a territory as big as Europe, is palpable. Were there ten thousand Apaches on the war-path, the task of hunting them down would be simple; but beside the catching of that handful, the proverbial needle in a haystack is a sinecure of discovery.

Not merely in size was (and is) his territory formidable, but still more in physical characteristics. Apachedom is a vast wilderness, and largely a vast desert— partially redeemable, and already dotted with semi-occasional oases. But I could lead you five hundred miles across it, in a not palpably circuitous line; and in all

that ghastly stretch you should not see one drop of
water save the precious fluid in our kegs. A desert,
truly, and a fearful one. Yet it is not a vast and
level sea of lifeless sands. It is, on the contrary, a
raggedly mountainous country ; and though sands
are plenty, they do not dominate the landscape. Upon
a vast, burnt-out plain, of undulant smoothness, a
multitude of wild peaks seem to have been flung down
superficially and hap-hazard. It is one of the features
of that unearthly landscape, that the mountains ap-
pear not to have grown from the bosom of the earth,
but to have been superimposed. There are no more
inhospitable and cruel peaks. Unkempt and dead and
shaggy with sharp crags and sharper cacti, they grin
down upon the circumfluent plain, by five hundred feet
to as many thousands. But two animals have ever
shone as successes in scaling these ragged peaks—
the cimarron and the Apache. The intervening valleys are equally characteristic. Melting in intangible
slopes, with the hazy smoothness of the Southwest,
accurst as the Sahara, thirsty as death on the battle-
field, nature has yet painted them with meretricious
gaudiness. A week after the rare rains, you shall
find square leagues carpeted with the Etruscan gold of
fragile Eschscholtzias, the snow of dainty marguerites,
the blood-red blotches of the *nopal*, and the varying
hues of many another flower. The gray-green of the
sage-brush, the greasewood's glaucous green, the
emerald daggers of the amole, the duller-hued bayonets of the aloe, topped with a banner of waxen white
—these are everywhere. And hither and yon tower
the giant candelabra of the zahuaro. But it is all a lie
and a cheat. There is no health in it. It is deadly

as the barren sands, that from a few miles away may
stretch for unbroken leagues.

That is our part of the favorite Apache range.
These impregnable peaks, these waterless and fiery
valleys, form such an "underground railway" as the
Kansas martyr never imagined.   Gifted with ordinary
secretiveness, one could slink from Colorado to the
safe wilderness of the Sierra Madre, by these Apache
trails, and never once be seen by human eye. Skulk-
ing through the rugged ranges by day, dashing across
the valleys by night, he could be as unobserved as
though he burrowed beneath the ground.   And even
should some casual hostile glance detect him, he has
but to scramble to yonder rocky crest, and he is safe.
There, amply supplied with ammunition, and absolutely unexposed, he could linger to slay as long as
pleased him, and then slip away by some cañon back-
door, and be off.

Such was the chief war-ground of the Apache.   Its
savage lord knew every foot of it better than you
know your own parlor.   Every water-pocket in the
mountains, every petty spring, every hollowed rock
wherein the rare rains might leave a life-giving drop
—all were his.   The white foe would die of thirst with·
in stone's-throw of the hidden water ; but no one ever
heard of an Apache perishing by the death of the
desert.   At every advantageous point he had a stronghold, where labor had supplemented nature, and
where spare arms and provisions might be *cachéd*.
He never went into camp, even for a night, without
fortifying his position.   A pursuer might pass within a hundred yards and never suspect ; but though
unobtrusive, the fortification was effective.

With such a country and such a knowledge of it, it is little wonder that the Apache was elusive. From the outstretched arm of pursuit he slid down into old Mexico as the picnic merrymaker comes down the greased pole, but with time to murder, rob, and ravish in transit. Safely ensconced in the vast and almost impenetrable wilderness of the Sierra Madre, he sallied out to some Mexican hamlet, sold his stolen stock, and bought ammunition and finery. Resting awhile in the mountains, he *cachéd* his most valuable plunder, looted perhaps the very village where he had been trading; and then, like a swart shadow, flitted back to his Arizona fastnesses. The condition of the hamlets which skirt the Mother Mountains was pitiful. The same atmosphere of terror was upon them as upon the Bengalese village around which the man-eater prowls. The outlying farms were swallowed up in jungles of cane; the very footfalls upon the street were nervous. The man of the house went to the spring with carbine in hand, and none ventured more than three or four miles from home. The relations of the Apache and the *paisano*—in Chihuahua, that is, for it was not so in Sonora—were peculiar; hostile always, bloody whenever occasion offered, yet comfortably commercial when a good round *peso* could be turned by either party. Nor did Chihuahua have a monopoly of this anomalous state of things. Many American merchants in Southern Arizona whose voices were loudest to have every Apache—man, woman, and child, hostile and friendly—exterminated, were at the same time selling whiskey, arms, and ammunition to the hostiles at much handsomer margins than lawful trade was wont to realize. The last six

months in which there were Apache horrors, were due
solely to an American trader who saw a diminution of
profits in a close of the war.   To avoid this danger, he intoxicated the Indians whose surrender had
ended the outbreak, and sent them out on the war-
path again.

The dress of the Apache warrior when upon the
reservation is a very gorgeous affair by comparison
with his campaign gear.   At home he affects as much
as possible the picturesque buckskin raiment, done
upon with fringe and silver and beadwork; and a
great array of aboriginal "jewelry."   But upon the
war-path he becomes a much soberer and more prac-
tical figure.

The average war-dress begins with a large and
aggressive-hued bandana—generally turkey-red or
orange-yellow—bound around the head from occiput
to sinciput.   It is designed to constrain the long,
dense hair, and to keep the sun from the eyes; but
its availability for decorative purposes is not dis-
dained, and it frequently bears one of the silver disks
so popular with all Southwestern tribes.

The ears are adorned invariably ; but, as a rule,
with less ponderous ear-rings than those worn at
home.   Sometimes they are strings of the valued turquoise ; but more often silver circlets.   The aged
Nanáy, Victorio's right-hand man, was inordinately
fond of wearing in either ear a huge gold watch-chain,
the cross-guard passed through a generous slit in his
ear, and eight or ten inches of heavy links depending.

A necklace of some sort is almost *de rigueur*,
though much greater plainness is permissible than at
home.   The average article is a yard-long string of

large glass beads, interspersed with magical berries
and roots, and with perhaps a few bits of turquoise.
One necklace is quite enough for the war-path, though
on the reservation a dozen are rather fashionable.

The shirt is of print, and generally of quiet hues,
for the loud colors cultivated at San Carlos would at-
tract entirely too much attention upon the war-path.
This thin upper garment is worn unsupplemented
alike in the one hundred and thirty degrees of the
summer desert and amid the snows of the Sierra
Blanca. Adept as is the Apache at all other ambus-
cades, it has never occurred to him to ambush the
extremities of his shirt; and they are left free to the
desert breeze. They conceal the commencement of
a pair of German linen drawers, designed to be
white, but of a present hue which is a monument to
the vanity of human hopes. The drawers, though
customary, are neither indispensable nor sufficient.
Those who chafe at their constraint violate no rules of
Apache etiquette in discarding them; but no one
may go, even upon the war-path, without the G-string.
This essential article of apparel—so named, probably,
because its convolutions somewhat resemble a capital
G—is in Apachedom a strip of unbleached muslin
about six feet long and two feet wide; and after it
has been knotted, the extremities form small aprons
in front and rear.

The war-moccasin is the most characteristic part of
the dress. It is made of heavy buckskin, sometimes
left in its natural soft gray, but more generally
stained a pleasant yellow. Instead of aspiring no
higher than the ankle—like the footgear of all the
northern tribes, and of the Apache himself when at

home—it has a leg three feet long but turned twice
over from the top, so that it reaches to the knee and
gives a triple armor over the whole calf and shin.
The toe does not end in the usual flat point, but
turns up at right angles in a round disk the size of a
half-dollar.   This disk is one with the rawhide sole.
The triple plating of the shin and the turn-up toe
are to circumvent the omnipresent and savage thorns
of the Apache's campaigning ground.

Rings and bracelets the warrior wears in plenty.
They are usually of silver or brass, though bead
bracelets are also sometimes used.   A little case of
aboriginal face-paint is always carried, and a small
mirror to guide the application of it in the proper
streaks, rings, blotches, and dots.   An awl encased
in leather, plenty of deer-sinew thread for mending
moccasins, tobacco and cigarette papers are also articles which every warrior keeps about him.   Besides
his rifle and six-shooter, with their belts of ammunition, he also has a butcher knife of Connecticut make.

With all this array, habitual in camp and on the
march, it is a singular fact that the Apache will never
fight in it save by compulsion.   Given two minutes'
notice of the proximity of a foe, he will enter the con-
flict as unencumbered as a Greek athlete.   He strips
off everything except the head-kerchief and the G-
string ; and takes his post behind some tiny shelter,
his bare hide indistinguishable, at a few yards' distance, from the brown earth.

Of the leaders in the last Apache war—the outbreak
of 1885–1886—a few words are in place.   Geronimo,
who enjoyed a rather undeserved newspaper notoriety
as the head and front of the entire outbreak, was no

chief. He rose to eminence by force of brains and jaw. Without the intellect of Chihuahua or Nanáy, he was a stronger talker than either of them, and had as powerful a will. His blood has been the theme of much fanciful fiction. There was an able and circumstantial story to the effect that he was a Mexican boy, captured by Victorio in 1852, in the little hamlet of Tumacacori, Sonora, and thereafter reared among the Apaches; and a dozen other stories as plausibly told. The fact, however, is, that Geronimo is a full-blooded Chihuicahui. He was in 1886 in the vicinity of forty-six years old; a compactly built, dark-faced man of 170 pounds, and about five feet eight inches in height. The man who has once seen his face will never forget it. Crueller features were never cut. The nose is broad and heavy, the forehead low and wrinkled, the chin full and strong, the eyes like two bits of obsidian with a light behind them. The mouth is the most noticeable feature—a sharp, straight, thin-lipped gash of generous length and without one softening curve. Geronimo has long been a prominent figure in Apachedom. When the Apaches were first put upon the reservation he was right-hand man to the famous Juh (pronounced Hoo). Naliza was also associated with them, and they made a gory trinity—Juh, the butcher; Geronimo, the organizer and plotter, and Naliza, the orator. When Juh stampeded first into Mexico, Geronimo went with him. In 1878 they surrendered (twenty-two bucks, 119 squaws and children) to Captain Haskell, and returned to the reservation. Geronimo stayed there quietly until 1881, when he accompanied Juh and all the rest of the Chihuicahuis into

Mexico again. Juh fell off a cliff while drunk and was drowned near Casas Grandes, Chihuahua. The rest remained in the wild Sierra Madre until the summer of 1883, when Crook brought back the whole 500 of them as the fruits of his brilliant campaign. From that time till the date of the last outbreak (May 17, 1885), Geronimo remained quietly upon the reservation, where he was generally unpopular on account of his overbearing and quarrelsome disposition.

Mangus, the prime mover in this outbreak, was a tall, finely formed fellow, perhaps forty years old. He was the son of the famous Mangus Colorado (Red Mangus), a giant of six-feet-seven, and as terrible as he was tall. Mangus had a very strong, resolute, and intelligent face, but showed no trace of the cunning ferocity so plainly stamped upon Geronimo's countenance. Mrs. Mangus, whose Apache name is Sago-zhu-ni (Pretty-mouth) brewed the tizwin by whose aid the eloquence of Mangus and Geronimo won their companions to the war-path.

Na-chi-ta, or "Natchez," a son of old Cochise, was the hereditary chief of the Chihuicahuis, and the "ranking officer" of the renegades. He was not a forceful character like his nominal subordinates, but a good-natured, vacillating fellow, fonder of wine and women than of war, but easily led by the nose by Geronimo. He was a tall, supple, graceful Indian, in his early thirties, with long, flexible hands, and a rather handsome but effeminate face. He stood five feet-eleven in his moccasins, and weighed 170 pounds. He went out in every raid since 1881.

Chihuahua was really the brainiest man and the strongest character among the Chihuicahuis. His

handsome, clean-cut, powerful face gave true index to
that behind. His countenance would be picked out
anywhere as a very kindly and benevolent one,
though pregnant with a reserved strength which
would warn an observant man not to impose upon
him. He was extremely fond of his bright children,
and had a kindly way with other people's youngsters.
But when Loco left the reservation in the spring of
1882, and a hated police officer attempted to inter-
fere, the aroused Chihuahua whacked off the med-
dler's head. Chihuahua was once a corporal of
scouts under Lieutenant Mills (Twelfth Infantry), and
did most effective service. His conduct on the reservation was exemplary. He devoted great care to his
farm, and would never have left had not the terrifying
lies of Geronimo fairly forced him into it. Chihuahua
was between forty-five and fifty years of age ; of
medium height and thick-set, muscular frame.

Old Nanáy was already superannuated, and ranked
mostly by his former glories. He was one of the
three chiefs of the Warm Springs Apaches, Victorio
and Loco being his associates. He was the brains
of the trinity, and almost as dreaded as Victorio, the
most terrible and most famous of Apaches. Nanáy's
last leadership of a raid was in the fall of 1881.
Since then he has merely " gone along " for company's sake. He was a short, fat, wrinkled old man
of fourscore years, leisurely in his movements, but
active upon occasion as a kitten. His face, far from
attractive, was the most impassive and undecipher-
able one of all—and that is saying a great deal.

Ulzanna, popularly corrupted to " Hosanna," was
not a chief, but an exceptionally active, keen, and

aggressive warrior of great prominence in his tribe. He was a scout with Chihuahua, and helped worry Nanáy terribly in 1881. Ulzanna led, in 1885, the bloodiest raid the Territories have known for years. He was about forty years old, of unpleasantly ferocious face and sturdy frame.

Kut-le, the bravest of the renegades, is another who achieved fame by his feats rather than his birth. He was a peculiar fellow, with a strong, massive face, great physical strength, boundless courage, and wonderful accuracy with the rifle. He was one of the six scouts who left Fort Thomas in 1881 and accompanied Juh.

When Crook, the grim, quiet soldier whom the Northern Indians called "the Grey Fox," and the Apaches Nan-tan-des-la-par-en, "Captain-with-the Brown-Clothes" (from his lack of peacock fondness for the insignia of rank) left Arizona for the rest well-earned by thirty-three years of hard campaigning—most of it on the frontier—the backbone of the Apache warrior was broken. Of the thirty-four men, eight well-grown boys, and ninety-two women and children who left the reservation on May 17, 1885, only twenty men and fourteen women were left upon the war-path. The rest were dead, or immured in a Florida prison. Geronimo and Nai-chi-ta were the only prominent men left with the renegades. Chihuahua, the smartest of them all; Old Nanay, the brains of Cochise; Ulzanna, the bloodiest and foxiest of raiders; Kut-le, the bravest Apache—all were prisoners in Fort Marion. The little band outstanding was disheartened and worn out by ceaseless pursuit. They wrote a few more bloody pages, as if for fitting finis to their ghastly record ; but it was their last gasp. General Miles continued Crook's tactics of ceaseless pursuit with the aid of Apache scouts—to whom the final suppression of the renegades is due—and at last the weary Geronimo and his men surrendered to the tireless Lawton and joined their brethren in Florida.

For a year and a half this handful of men—thirty-four warriors at the most, and later but twenty—encumbered by thrice their number of women, children, and babes, defied, and successfully defied, the power of a nation of 60,000,000 people, not to mention Mexico. For every man the hostiles lost they killed twenty-five. They travelled such distances as no army in the whole world's history ever approximated, and endured such privations as would have killed any other men. In this campaign more than in any of its predecessors they showed not only marvellous courage and endurance, but wonderful generalship.

That is the Apache warrior—unpalliated and un-gilded—or rather, that he was, so long as there was an Apache warrior. The superb campaigns and management of General Crook, with the finishing touches added by General Miles, ended the Chihuicahui as a warlike factor, in 1886. Nothing but wanton abuse could again drive him upon the war-path. He is now a peaceful farmer, learning the lessons of civilization as fast as aboriginal man can learn them—much faster than the Saxon cave-dweller learned them. But it is worth while to preserve this leaf from the past which made him famous—the past in which he rose to be the most perfect warrior.

VIII

ON THE TRAIL OF THE RENEGADES

ON THE TRAIL OF THE RENEGADES

1886.

HIGH noon in southern Arizona. The sun is a flood of infinite fire, wherein earth and sky are saturated. The heavens are an arch of burnished brass. The blinding landscape seems the thin crust over a sea of boiling lava—as if white-hot from inner fires. Great billows of heat, palpable as smoke, waver up from its broad bosom. If such a thing as shade were conceivable there, the mercury would stand at 135° beneath it; on that bare sand the heat beats down with indescribable intensity. Touch a palm to that sand, and you shall acquire blisters as from a red-hot stove. The panting jack rabbit lies outstretched behind a fortuitous bushlet, careless of human propinquity. The birds which will be abroad at sunset are absolutely gone. There is no moving thing but the sinuous lizards, which flash jerkily from sand-hole to sand-hole, in salamandrine heedlessness of the awful glow. There is no faintest sound of life. No breeze stirs the rare and tiny bushes to whispering coquetries.

There *is* life all about, but for now in lethargy. Down in the hollow yonder, dark forms, prone and motionless, dot the sand. There are patches of the familiar blue; and blinding glints waver on some-

thing beside them.   One, two, three, four—they are
an even hundred men.   Their heads are covered with
heavy blankets; and each is behind a greasewood
whose shade might equal that of a hollyhock.   Their
legs and bodies project into the fiery glow, and you
note that but twenty of them wear boots.   All the
rest are furnished as to the feet with the pug-nosed
moccasin which the Apache wears upon the war-path.
There are twenty pairs of light blue trousers, ten
pairs of grimy linen drawers, and seventy pairs of
legs as bare and swart as a Bushman's.   Here and
there, too, from under some head-muffling blanket
straggle heavy locks of long, black hair.

Not many rods away from these recumbent figures
is another group, numerically equal, but socially less
—the mules of the pack-train.   Poor patient brutes!
They stand in semicircular rank, with heads all toward the centre, their big ears drooping, their fitful
tails motionless.   They do not bray, nor move a muscle; but with heads dependent and backs to the sun,
stand there awaiting with confidence the fall of night.
They are too old campaigners to complain.   In a
regular row behind them are the *aparejos* and the
packs.   There, too, are the bearded and dusty packers, with each his head poked beneath a saddle.   And
from all this there is no sound of life.

The skeleton shadows of the greasewood and the
mescal grow longer.   The few tall candelabra of the
giant-cactus turn dark against the southern sky.
Songless birds flit here and there.   The long-legged
jack rabbit stretches, erects himself to an interrogative
perpendicular, and then lopes easily off across the
plain.   A lizard flirts into his hole just in advance of

a suddenly interested owl ; and the mules voice their tardy content in hysterical laughter.

It is sunset. Do not fancy thereby that it is cool. The mercury would still notch 120°—but for awhile it *seems* cool. That terrific glare is gone, and the throbbing eyes are grateful. A faint breeze falters across the still ardent sands—its breath the breath of a furnace, but welcome contrast to that fiery stagnation. The mules break their regular alignment and yield themselves to the untender hands of the packers, who have crawled from beneath the saddles with limp profanity. There is life, too, among the recumbent hundred. The head - muffling blankets are thrown off, and the bodies assume the perpendicular in various degrees of unhaste. There is general stretching of legs and arms, much vague cursing, and a unanimous rally to the water-kegs.

And now we may note the personnel of the command—Captain ——'s expedition in pursuit of Geronimo and his co-renegades. There is the captain himself—a tall, broad-shouldered, youngish Saxon of tawny hair and beard ; his two lieutenants, rather younger ; the surgeon, a quiet, unruffled German ; the chief of scouts, a brawny, clear-eyed Missourian of twenty years' hardening upon the frontier ; the chief packer and fifteen white soldiers of the regular army. It is noticeable how all of them are of superb physique—bronzed, deep-throated, broad-chested, and clean-limbed. They are trained athletes every one, picked for their task.

Near them, yet retaining a general differentiation, is the real strength of the expedition—the company of Apache scouts. You may well study them. Just such a contingent was perhaps never seen in war outside the incomparable campaigns inaugurated by Crook in the Southwest.   There are eighty of them ; straight, swarthy, tireless sons of the desert—the only human beings capable of catching their renegade brethren.   Here is Sergeant Noche, an intelligent-looking Chihuicahui of about thirty-eight years, built like an Apollo, and dressed in the full uniform of his rank.   Here also is Sergeant Charlie, who wears the blouse and chevrons of Uncle Sam, but the nether garb of Apachedom.   Here, in full Apache outfit, is Dutchy—a yellow, evil-faced Chihuicahui, of whose traits his own *compadres* show their appreciation by calling him Yellow Coyote.   He is a dangerous fellow, and has killed several whites ; but his energy, acuteness, and experience make him a most valuable scout.   He proves the maxim " Set a thief to catch a thief."   Among his companions are representatives of half a dozen Apache tribes ; the Chihuicahuis predominating, and the Warm Springs, White Mountains, Tontos, and Mojaves following in that order.   Nearly all wear army blouses ; some have drawers of unbleached German linen ; but most have nothing below the waist except the inevitable G-string and the high-topped moccasins.   It is not a bad-looking crowd, though one wherein the observant would scarce " pick a muss."   Great good-nature prevails as the brown soldiers cluster around hasty fires of the greasewood's ardent roots and cook the simple meal of jerked venison.   At the fire with Noche and Dutchy is a notable figure—a wee, shrivelled but well-proportioned person whose age might be forty or one hundred, so far as his face or figure tell.   His form is wiry, his features thin, clear-cut, and intelligent. His hair is long, jet, and straight as an Indian's, and his color is to match. But he is no Indian. This is Concepcion, the Mexican chief-interpreter. He has passed his life with the Apaches, who captured him in boyhood and reared him as one of themselves. He was an apt pupil. He loves to tell of the raids, the robberies, and the butcheries in which he has participated, and always winds up with: " *Oh, yo era muy diablo* " (I was very much a devil)—a proposition to which his eyes give full credibility.

The beans, the bacon, and the hard-tack have come to grief; the pack-saddles and packs are cinched tightly upon their patient wearers, and the command is ready to move. The full, red moon floats above the horizon, lending new unearthliness to the weird landscape. Dutchy's quick eye detects a small, dark spot far down the valley. No Caucasian can see it for fifteen minutes yet; but all lay down their guns to await developments. In half an hour is heard the crunch of horse-hoofs upon the crisp sand; and in a few minutes more a travel-stained courier dismounts from his lathered brute and hands an official envelope to the captain. It is a message from Crook. The renegades have been seen the day before in the Chihuicahui Mountains; they were heading south toward Mexico.

The order to march is given instantly; and in five minutes the long procession is stringing southeastwardly down the ghostly valley; the pack-train dangling in the rear, while the scouts push ahead and to either flank in groups, which become more and more scattered as the night wears on. Midnight

13

comes ; one o'clock, two o'clock, three o'clock.   The
caravan is now fifteen miles long, if you count from
extreme rear to extreme front, though the bulk of it is
within three miles.   The main force is still skirting
the fringes of the lofty Chihuicahui range, whose
peaks shoot far into the mellow ether, moonlit and
sublimated.   The scouts are sprinkled ahead, with
twenty of them rayed out in fan-fashion many miles
to the fore.   Some are far out on the broad, fair plain
of Sulphur Springs Valley; others have skipped up
the rocky peaks like so many goats, and are ransack-
ing every ravine, while a few are skirmishing about
the very summit, watching for the distant signal-fires
of the wily foe.   The atmosphere has become cool—
that is to say, the temperature is not to exceed one
hundred degrees.   I hardly need mention that the
heat of Arizona is not like the heat of Missouri or
New York.   The glow of the desert is dry and
withering, with none of that muggy, exhausting
quality of Eastern summers.   One hundred and ten
degrees is no more felt in Arizona than eighty degrees in the valley of the Mississippi, except by
the eyes.

At four o'clock the soldiers are climbing the steep
approach to a pass whereby the range is to be
crossed ; and an hour later are building the breakfast
fires in a wide angle of the cañon, whence their glow
will tell no tales to savage eyes across the broad valley of the San Simon.   It is a fascinating outlook
which this lofty station commands as the sky flashes
into dawn.   Four thousand feet below is the great
valley, stretching away to the blue hills of New Mexico on the east; and south to the hazy ranges of

Old Mexico. Northeast the Stein's Peak range walls the plain; and a trifle northwest of it rise the mountainous tiers which culminate upon the horizon with the superb Sierra Blanca, one hundred and twenty-five miles away. Over all is that peculiarly fascinating haze, dreamy and magical, which invests the arid countries of the Southwest, and gives them a soft sensuousness, a weird beauty to which the fairest and most fertile regions of the East are strangers.

After breakfast and a short rest, the march is resumed, the course taken after leaving the cañon and descending to the plain being in a general south-southwesterly direction. The course is thus far a merely tentative one, for the field - glasses which swept the landscape while yet upon the mountain disclosed no sign of the foe. All day long the steady trudge, trudge, trudge continues. It is a fearful experience—such an experience as the three Hebrews in their fiery furnace may have known. The blinding glare, the terrific heat, the molten sand; the clouds of alkaline dust which rise from every footstep and crawl lazily aloft, filling eyes, nose, throat and lungs with torture—who that is of the little band will ever forget these? And what cataclysm shall efface the memory of that thirst, which walked with each like a consuming flame, which paralyzed tongue and throat, eradicated the voice and shrivelled the lips to leather?

So the day wears off. The breathless but more merciful night comes down and brings brief respite. The main command is now near an inferior range; and a handful of the tireless scouts scatter up the darkening slopes, while the Caucasians sink to the ground to snatch a bit of sleep. How log-like that rest is, despite the stifling heat and the roughness of the couch, and unrefreshing as log-like. One arises from it still soaked in lethargy, and for hours afterward trudges on as in a trance.

This nap is a short one. It is eleven o'clock when a tall, supple figure comes into camp on a quick trot and shakes the captain by the shoulder. This scout and his companions have been to the top of the range, whence they saw a fire some twenty miles to the southeast. It was too broad, too high, and too long-lived for a signal-fire, and they take it to be the burning of some building. The others have pushed on to reconnoitre, while Bi·er·le brings back the news. His message acts like an electric shock. In five minutes every man in the force is afoot: in twenty minutes all are moving up the long, smooth slope toward the range; while the pack-train with a little escort turns off down the valley to the south, with orders to meet at Lang's Ranch.

Toiling up the steep mountain side, straggling down the opposite slope, crossing valleys and hills, barrancas and ridges, they follow the lead of Bi·er·le all the weary night. As the sky quickens to pearly dawn he points to a thin, dark line of smoke stringing ominously upward. They cross the last divide, and look down into the smiling valley. A ribbon of vivid green down the hillside bespeaks the presence of spring; and beside it are the tokens of human occupancy. In that land of thirst the tiny cienega is more than a gold-mine; and by this one a hardy German had established his little cattle rancho and built his modest 'dobe home. When it was done, he had brought over from Tucson his buxom wife and tow-haired baby, and there they had lived, "the world forgetting, by the world forgot."

But that is not what the men see as they run down the hill and stop panting among the scouts, who have been waiting there for hours. The adobe walls are there, but bare and blackened. Their thatch has gone up in smoke, and only ashes mark where stood the wagons and the stacks of hoe-mown hay. Scattered here and there are the carcasses of half a dozen cattle, from which small chunks of meat have been cut. Around the corner of the ruined house is the stalwart ranchero, stretched upon the ground. A big, rough stake, split from his own wagon, is driven through his abdomen and deep into the hard earth. The poor eyeballs, gouged from their sockets, have been replaced wrong-side out. The ears are pinned to either side of the nose with cactus thorns. There are other mutilations which no pen dare tell. A few yards away lies the little frau, staked down by wrists and ankles, the victim of a thousand deaths; and across her poor clay the body of her babe.

The scouts have read from the tracks that the hostiles number twenty warriors, with twenty-five women and children—a strong party. From other indications it is believed that the band is Geronimo's own. There is no more thought of rest, though the march already has been exhausting, and the heat is unabated. The majority of the scouts are already miles ahead upon the easily followed trail. The white contingent is an hour late in starting, and leaves behind it two decent mounds, with a rough board at the head of each. The march is rapid but moody. There is little conversation, and a general irritability is evident. A stub of the toe brings a snarl of profanity, entirely disproportionate, from the victim, while his companions act as though he had no business to be so clumsy. One would fancy he had done violence to their toes instead of his own. Everyone is out of sorts —the usual careless cheeriness is gone.

The trail indicates that the hostiles have made a straight shoot for their fastnesses far below the Mexican line, and arrangements are made accordingly. The trail is dropped, and the command switches across to the supply-camp at Lang's Ranch, in the extreme southwest corner of New Mexico. Here a day goes in fitting out for a long campaign. The instructions from General Crook are: "Pursue with utmost vigor, regardless of department or national boundaries." That means that it may be three months before the company again sees United States soil. The pack-train has got in ahead, having taken a much shorter route. The packers are carefully overhauling their appurtenances, and paying particular attention to their animals. These long-eared plodders carry the lives of the command, and they earn a respect not everywhere given them. The chief packer of the department, veteran Tom Moore, has his own ideas about them. Says he:

"People disparage the mule because they do not know him. He is no accident. *God made the mule on purpose.* The horse has that in him which shows he was meant for something more than a mere slave. Man needed a straight-out servant, and so God built him the mule. And a true servant he is, from the time he begins to walk until the breath leaves his worn-out shell. You might almost say he is useful every day of his life. He is always faithful and always reliable if rightly treated. He knows his business, and does it as few men do theirs. It is an idiocy to curse and club him. Any man in my train who does it, gets his walking papers."

The lieutenant who acts as quartermaster replenishes the commissary from the supply depot. The scouts are busy, too. With awls and deer-sinew thread they patch their moccasins, or supplant an attenuated sole with a new piece of rawhide, with the hair down. This done, they proceed to the no less exigent duty of personal decoration for the war-path. With a generous tallow shampoo they mollify their great shocks of bushy hair, till it is sleek and obedient. Next in order comes attention to the complexion. A few of the more fastidious have with them little packages of American dry paint, mostly vermilion. The ordinary face-powder, however, is more simple of acquirement. Some colored rock is pulverized and mixed with grease to the consistency of salve ; after which it is artistically applied with the middle or forefinger of the right hand, a little mirror being used as a guide to the proceeding. Some of the more fanciful have selected a blue micaceous stone, whose dust glitters weirdly upon their swart faces. Others, who have killed a *conejo* or a deer, have drawn across the face, from ear to ear, an inch-wide band of blood. But the artists of the whole band are two coffee-coolers,* who have found a wayside vein of green copper-ore, and have bedaubed their faces with its tallowed powder, while a trans-nasal stripe of vermilion gives the finishing touch. The green has the

---

* Lazy and inferior scouts.

most ghastly effect conceivable; and has converted two rather tame-looking aborigines into the most cut-throat-looking pirates that ever trod the earth.

It is a day less fiery than its predecessors as the command files out of Lang's Ranch, crosses the national boundary line, and plunges into the inhospitable depths of the step-sister republic. In a few miles it meets Bi-er-le and his detachment, who have been reconnoitring the trail of the renegades. They have followed it for fifty miles, to learn the probable destination of the hostiles, and then come back to bring such information as they have gathered—which is to the general effect that the hostiles have scooped in an abundance of good stock and miscellaneous plunder, and are moving leisurely southwest.

The command pushes forward as rapidly as may be through the Sierra Média, over Dos Carretas Creek, and thus across the northwestern corner of the great Mexican State of Chihuahua; thence down deep into Sonora, past the little towns of Bavispe, Basserac and Guachineva to Huepere Creek, one hundred and seven miles from Lang's. Here it is the intention to rest a day, as the hard marching has told on the white men and pack animals; but a tattered and greasy mail-carrier brings a note which denies this pleasant recess. The prefect of the Montezuma district informs by these presents that there has been a large band of Apaches, mostly women and children, operating in that vicinity, and that the citizens of Oposura have followed them from the Sonora River over to the Terez Mountains. It is dusk when this news comes; and at midnight all are again under way, little rested, but hopeful of a brush with the elusive foe. After a

long, hard scramble over the Huepere, Madera, and
Oputo Mountains, six o'clock the next evening finds
the company going into camp six miles north of
Oputo. The *Presidente* of that hamlet declares that
the chase is getting warm. He only wishes they had
arrived twenty-four hours earlier. That very day the
hostiles have fired upon farmers fifteen miles north,
killing one man and running off some stock. An hour
later, just as the sun is going down, twenty-six excited
Oputans come into camp, and with an avalanche of
gestures promulgate that they have been chasing
these hostiles, and saw them kill a beef and take it
into the Joya Mountains. The command is dead
weary—the white contingent, that is—and positively
unable to move further without some rest. The scouts,
however, are fresh as daisies; and as soon as night
drops her curtains, six of these are sent out to sneak
into the Joya and locate the hostile camp. Before
daylight next morning all are off and march down to
a point a mile below Oputo, where they camp in a
concealed position, and lie close all day. At eight
o'clock in the evening two of the six scouts come in.
They have trailed up the hostiles into the mountains,
at a respectful distance and watched for detailed information from a commanding point. They saw the
hostile squaws gathering mescal for a grand mescal-
bake, and by closely watching their movements have
learned that the camp is located upon the highest
peak of the Joya. They have come to tell, leaving
the other four to watch. This is good news. Every
ear is pricked up, and every eye sparkles. It looks,
as though there were after all to be a "whack" at
these evasive wretches. At midnight, leaving the en-

tire pack-train under guard, and personally carrying
two days' rations, they march across atrociously
rough country till daylight, which finds them nine
miles north of Oputo. Here at the first streaks of
dawn, they conceal themselves in the timber—for they
are now in a well-watered and wooded country, a
smiling contrast to the hideous desert left behind—
and lie there through the whole day, passing the hours
as well as may be. It is not exactly a hilarious time.
Cooking is interdicted, and there will hardly be another fire so long as they are in Mexico. Hunting
is also out of the question; nor will it do to move
about promiscuously, for any slightest exposure is
liable to be noted by the concealed savage upon yonder peak, who is even now sweeping the country with
as fine a pair of field-glasses as the United States
affords. So the day passes tediously enough. The
scouts amuse themselves playing *con quien* for one
another's cartridges. The white soldiers as a rule
sleep sonorously beneath the grateful shade—for the
weather is still like the hinges of Hades. In the afternoon all the scouts are sent out to join the four who
have been all this time watching the hostile camp.
They drop their blankets, grasp their rifles, and slink
away through the barrancas and mesquite thickets
like grim, dark shadows. At 7 P.M. the entire command follows, marching silently through the gathering darkness, and spreading out more and more as
they cut down the nine miles between them and the
mountain, whose great dark bulk looms upon the
starry sky. Before the east shows a sign of waken-
ing day, a cordon of grimly eager men is drawn entirely around the peak, about a mile below its summit.

As day breaks there is cautious advance up the rugged
steep, the furtive scouts in the lead slipping from bush
to bush, from rock to sheltering rock, never exposed,
never at a loss. The silence is ominous. The men
nervously hold their thumbs upon the hammer and
poke their guns before them as they worm up the
breathless acclivity. And still no sound—till suddenly
Noche, who has been snaking far ahead upon his
belly, leaps to his feet upon the rocky summit with a
howl of rage, which is echoed from every throat as
the rest rush forward to find themselves in a deserted
camp, bare as a bird's foot. Those ineffable dodgers,
seeing troops in the Oputa Valley, and knowing that
there are Chihuicahui scouts along as acute as themselves, have slunk from their camp at about the same
time the force started from the foot of the mountain.
They are now thirty or forty miles away. It is an
occasion which tests the profane ability of every pursuer, and oaths of every description—English, Spanish, and choice Chihuicahui—fill the air. There is little
comfort in the fact—read by the scouts from tatters of
the women's dresses found on the thorns—that the
band was Geronimo's very own.

While half-a-dozen scouts follow up the trail of the
renegades, others are sent back to pilot the pack-
train, and the command moves quietly down to the
swift Bavispe River, camping in the dense canebrakes
at the mouth of the San Juan and there awaiting the
pack-train, which comes up on the second day. One
of the scouts, who was with the hostiles in the last
outbreak, knows a large spring on the eastern slope
of La Joya, where the *mescal* grows in great abundance. It is a favorite resort of the renegades, who

frequently camp there six or seven days at a time for a grand mescal-roast. In hope that they may now do so, seventy-six of the best scouts, with five days' short-rations, are sent thither, while the rest of the command moves down to Bavispe, across the mountains and on to Huepere Creek. The scouts are there ahead, with good news. Bi·er·le, with a few Coyotero scouts, has surprised a small band of hostiles and bushwhacked them commendably, killing two of them and capturing four horses, three saddles, three bridles, and three blankets. This is an important "action" for an Apache war.

The trail of the renegades now bends south toward the Sierra Madre, and seventy-eight scouts are sent in pursuit under a lieutenant and two chiefs-of-scouts (white men) ; while the rest of the command stays in camp near Huepere, awaiting the return of the pack-train which has been sent to Lang's Ranch for supplies. A week later, the seventy-eight scouts surprise Geronimo's camp thirty miles north-northeast of Nacori, in a mountainous stronghold. A surprise means here not exactly what it would in civilized warfare. It is merely that the pursuers get within a few hundred yards of the pursued before they are detected ; that they catch a few running shots at elusive figures which melt behind bush and rock like so many phantoms, swap lead awhile and are off—leaving to the foe such impediments as cannot handily be carried away. Upon the present occasion the scouts, by infinite work and strategy, crawling bellywise all night along the rough ground, came very close upon Geronimo's camp. At five hundred yards one of the hostiles heard an unfortunate twig snap, and the stalk

was up.   From answering rock to rock the bullets
pattered.   The scouts, stripping off every rag save
the G-string, crawled forward from cover to cover,
firing as they went.   The hostiles retrograded in the
same fashion ; and when the assaulting party reached
their empty camp, they had maintained their distance, or, perhaps, gained a little.   The fight is an
unusually one-sided one.   Not a man of the pursuers
is hurt save the lieutenant, whose Caucasian tactics
were not sufficiently secretive, and whose shoulder
has suffered serious boring.   But in the hostile camp
and the next half mile of pursuit are found the bodies
of three warriors, one squaw, one eleven-year-old
boy, and a nursing baby—the usual fortune when it
comes to a fight.

The lieutenant's shoulder is bandaged, the corpses
are left to the coyotes for interment, and the men follow the scouts, who have pressed on in running pursuit.   In the race that afternoon they capture all the
laggards of the foe—fifteen squaws and children, thirteen horses and mules, the blankets, saddles, and entire camp-outfit, including a few battered pots, some
jerked meat, and a large quantity of roasted *mescal*.
Among the captured children is one big-headed, wide-
eyed, handsome boy-baby—Little Robe, a son of
Geronimo.*

The hostiles gain thirty miles a day ; and detailing
a dozen scouts to keep posted as to their general
course, the command camps on the third day to await
the arrival of the replenished pack-trains ; upon their

---

* This little fellow with his mother was taken to Fort Bowie, and was a great
pet at the guard-house there for several months.   He died there September 10,
1885, and was buried in the lonely little graveyard below the fort.

coming, to push on again into the wild and lonely south.

For the next three weeks there is little to record, save the monotonous and unresting pursuit. There is news of the hostiles, now and then, in terrorized hamlets. There has been a swoop down upon their herds, all the best stock has been swept away and the *vaqueros* slain. That is about all they know. They have not been particular about following the marauders, who have gone " three days to the south." In all these towns are met dislike ; in the larger ones, undisguised hostility. In Basserac, the alcade tries to shoot Dutchy and a couple of his companions, out of mere wantonness. Anything American is as hated as the Apaches themselves—perhaps more so. These *paisanos* are not, however, above making a *peso* out of the common foe ; and despite the utmost vigilance they are constantly bringing out *mescal* and *pulque* through the bushes to the scouts. The blouses and the chevrons and the $13 per month are all very good in their way, but they are only a veneer of discipline. No power could make a band of Apaches march in rank or column ; it is a physical impossibility to watch that two-mile procession so closely that the ardent will not leak in.

News from the *Presidente* of Granadas, and from General Guerra—a commander in the regular Mexican army, who is out with five hundred men in pursuit of the broncos *—tells that there have been depradations near Toni-babi, up among the Oposura Mountains ; and thither the force hastens. Southeast of Tepache they " cut " (intersect) a hot trail, and

* Frontierism for hostile Apaches as distinguished from Apache scouts.

follow it, without rest or food, to the top of rugged
Mount Salitral. Long before, however, the hostiles
have become aware of the pursuit. The lookout,
whom they invariably leave from five to twenty miles
in the rear, armed with the finest of field-glasses, has
"spotted" the pursuers, who gain the mountain-top
less than an hour behind the foe ; and stumble upon
the carcasses—some still warm—of thirty horses and
burros which they have stabbed and abandoned upon
finding the pursuit too hot. They are scattered now
like quail among the rocks, all afoot. Their trail is
almost undiscernible, even to the hawk-like eyes
which are bent above it. Sergeant Cooley (Apache)
and nineteen scouts push ahead of all the rest, using
the utmost caution. Within twenty miles they overtake the rear-guard of the hostiles and capture their
blankets. Cooley and his brother imprudently hurry
on, and half a mile later literally walk into an ambush.
A bullet fired ten feet away pierces the heart of Cooley's brother, and Cooley saves himself only by a
lightning drop behind a rock. There is a general
running fight from that on till dark. One of the
scouts gets a bullet in his thigh, and one bronco is
left to fester behind his fortress rock. Several more
hostiles are more or less wounded, judging by the
gory bandages and blood-drops found on the trail
next day.

So it goes. For every shot at a hostile the pursuers travel two hundred miles over the roughest,
wildest, most forsaken country on the face of the
globe ; consumed by sultry heat ; devoured at night
by myriads of atrocious insects ; too tired and hot to
relish the greasy fare of bacon and heavy bread ;

with sore and sometimes bleeding feet; with clothing soaked for days at a time by tremendous rains which obliterate every trail. From the time of crossing the Mexican line until the return to the United States they do not see a post-office, telegraph-office, or railroad. They are as much shut off from the world as though midway on a journey to the moon. To-day they chase a rumor east and to-morrow double westward on it. And all this time that matchless foe is having much his own way.

Between Nacosari and Cumpas there is a diversion. While following a trail of Chihuahua's band—which has just gathered in all the valuable horses from the American Ranch—the command comes upon an American man and woman concealed in a ravine. The woman has a cartridge-belt around her waist, in one hand a Winchester, and in the other a double-barrelled shot-gun. And she means business. Woe to the foremost scout if she had not seen in time his regulation blouse! She has a stirring story to tell. Yesterday afternoon a band of hostiles attacked her party—four men and herself—on their way from Tombstone *via* Nacosari to some mines in the Nacosari Mountains. One American was killed at the first fire, and two others ran for dear life, leaving their companion to shift for herself. One man stayed with her, apparently because he was too frightened to run. But the plucky woman was equal to the occasion. Running to the body of the dead man under fire, she grabbed the shot-gun from his hands, a belt of cartridges from his waist, and the Winchester from his mule, and opened on the foe. One of the hostiles still carries a buckshot which she tucked under his

tawny hide. She "stood off" the raiders, and re-
treated in good order with her companion—leaving
all their burros and effects, however, in the enemy's
hands. Later in the day was found the body of the
dead American, and beside it the four empty shot-gun
cartridges used by gritty Belle Davis, of Tombstone,
in her fight for life. The two Americans who ran
away were never heard more of. Let us trust that
the Apaches caught and toasted them.

It were needless to detail more of the expedition.
The middle chapter is like the first, the last like the
middle. The chase leads hither and yon over the
untenanted plains and ineffably rugged mountains,
in doublings, loops, and many an elusive maze. It is
followed until the very scouts are worn out—their
moccasons in rags ,their feet cut and swollen, and
their temper inflamed. The white men of the party,
who have not travelled one-half so far, are nearly
dead of fatigue. The commissary is again running
low, and the enlistment of the scouts will be out in
ten days. So when they have followed a small trail
up through Guadalupe cañon and lost it close to the
national line, they meet a courier from headquarters
with orders to proceed to Fort Bowie, leaving the
pursuit to Captain ——, who takes it up as they de-
part.

Then comes the weary tramp up the arid valleys of
Arizona, and on the ninetieth day they file down the
winding path through Apache Pass, in upon the
steeply sloping parade-ground of Fort Bowie. The
paymaster has just arrived. The scouts are paid off
next day, and "blow themselves in" at Delong's sut-
ler's store, whence they emerge resplendent in new

14

bandana handkerchiefs, gay Mexican *zarapes*, and many a foolish trinket.   As next morning's sun fires the Chihuicahui peaks, the wild procession of scouts —now mounted on hardy little ponies of their own— files out through the notch into the bare, broad plain, and is off for Fort Apache, at the reservation, where they will be disbanded.   The old fort sinks back to sleepiness broken only by the daily routine of discipline, and men eat and sleep hard—resting for a while from that three months' taste of life on an Apache trail.

Fort Bowie was built here in 1862 by the California Volunteers.   Three-quarters of a mile west, on a pretty little bench above the wash, stands the graveyard, within a high picket fence.   Its white headboards gleam in the eternal sun, and doves coo upon the narrow mounds.   Between its ridges the ground is gay with golden wild poppies and snowy margrites ; and here and there, upon some less-neglected grave a buckhorn cactus spreads its prickly antlers, or a turk's head nestles close to the bare gravel. There are but two memorial stones in the whole enclosure ; all the other head-boards are of pine, planed and painted white, while cramped black letters in straggling lines tell their terse story.   All burying-grounds cover that which was once life and hope and love ; but this lonely half-acre along the barren hillside of Apache Pass is eloquent with the story of the Arizona frontier.   It is full of Apache workmanship. The dumb upheavals of its brown breast tell of the old stage creaking up the desolate cañon ; the sudden little puff from behind yon innocent tuft of beargrass, matched by another from that rock, and another from the aloe-bunch beyond; the sturdy driver tumbling from his perch; the tangled horses floundering in terror; the ashen passenger dragged from his concealment; and last of all a horrid bonfire whose smoke goes up with sickening smells and shrieks.

There are thirty-three graves whose head-boards record simply that: " —— died on the —th of ——, 18—." Of these, seven were children. The presumption is that they passed away in the course of nature. Another board is so weathered that it no longer tells what may lie beneath.

One of the first graves as one enters is that, so the board says, of

O. O. SPENCE.

Born in Pennsylvania.

Killed by Indians, April 7, 1876.

Close beside it is a broad wooden cross, along whose arms runs the legend, in ornate letters,

NICHOLAS M. ROGERS.

Born in St. Joseph, Mo.

Killed by Indians, April 7, 1876.

Next it in the line stands one to the memory of

JOHN McWILLIAMS.

Killed by Apaches, Feb. 26, 1872.   Aged 26.

Beyond is a wider mound, whose board tells of

A. F. BICE, F. PETTY, F. DONOVAN.

Killed by Indians in Apache Pass, Jan. 24, 1872.

Next comes a board bearing the simple inscription:

IN MEMORY OF
COL. STONE.
Supposed to be.

That last line is a whole page of the frontier. Colonel Stone had a mine on the hills just back of the fort. One day he disappeared, and searchers found only a mass of meat, hacked past recognition, but "supposed to be" the missing miner. There are other similar guess - work graves — "Lieut. Julian Agueira, supposed to be;" "James McIntyre, supposed to be;" "John Kilbey, supposed to be."

Another head-board says:

IN MEMORIAM OF
GEO. KNOWLES,
Prvt. Co. H., 32 U. S. Inf., captured and tortured to death by Apache Indians, May 26, 1868.

Knowles and another private named King were acting as guards to the stage down the pass. Just before they reached the plain, the stage was "jumped" by Apaches, and the driver instantly killed. The conductor, who was known here as " Tennessee," " stood off" the foe for a while, but was soon wounded and overcome. For some reason the Apaches did not butcher him, but carried him off captive. He was afterward killed in Mexico in a fight between the Apaches and Mexicans. The two soldiers do not appear to have made any resistance—no empty shells from their guns could be found. They probably threw up their hands and surrendered. Poor fools!

Their captors bound and roasted them alive, with variations.

In the northeast corner of the yard are two tiny mounds, side by side. One head-board says:

> IN MEMORY OF
> LITTLE-ROBE,
> SON OF
> GERONIMO,
> APACHE CHIEF.
> Died Sept. 10, 1885;
> Age two years.

The other:

> IN MEMORY OF
> MARCIA,
> AN APACHE CHILD,
> Died July 3, 1885;
> Age three years.

It was a soldierly and a manly heart which cared that these poor little captive waifs had decent burial, and that their last resting-place was decently marked. It would hardly have befallen so, in those days and that part of Arizona, outside of army circles.

Besides the victims above recorded of Apache bullet and knife, the following names are on other boards in this quiet ground, each with the ominous line, " Killed by Apaches: "

LIEUT. JOHN C. CARROLL, 32nd Infantry, Nov. 5, 1867.
SAMUEL HICKMAN, Private, Troop F, Fourth Cav., Oct. 10, 1885.
JOHN M. COSS.
JOHN F. KEITH, June 25, 1862.
PETER R. MALONEY, 1st Cav., California Vols., June 25, 1862.
ALBERT SCHMIDT, June 25, 1865.

CASSIUS A. B. FISHER, formerly of 1st Inf., California Volunteers, Feb. 19, 1867.

JOHN BROWNLEY, May 26, 1868.

There are fourteen other graves whose head-boards bear the pregnant line,

"UNKNOWN,"

and eleven unmarked mounds. A fair record, that, for the little area almost within gun-shot of the fort. It is one short page of the Apache's incomparable autograph book.

IX

NEW MEXICAN FOLK-SONGS

NEW MEXICAN FOLK-SONGS*

FOR seven years I have been collecting the folk-songs of the Spanish and Indian Southwest. The acquisition of several thousand of these quaint ditties has been no small labor. They had never been written out, but were preserved by oral transmission, like the Indian folk-lore, and without the remarkable exactness which the ceremonial nature of the latter secures. To get the entire words of a song was therefore sometimes a matter of *trailing* them through the mouths of scores of singers, a territory asunder. Most difficult of all was it to get the music correctly. Aside from the characteristic idiosyncrasies of these airs—their unique rhythm with strange swings and rests and runs—there was an ever-present obstacle in the deficiency of the teacher. There everybody sings, and almost nobody *can* sing. Out of this great collection of songs, acquired from hundreds of different sources, I learned less than a score from persons who had any remotest understanding of music. There was but one way to get an air. A phonograph would have scared off my bashful troubadours, even if it could have caught—as no portable phonograph yet devised could catch, with its varying

---

* For the very accurate transcription of the airs of these songs I am indebted to the young American composer, Henry Holden Huss. In the words accompanying the music I have accented the words which have to be mispronounced to meet the stress of the song.

register—the unique *movimiento* which is the heart
of that music.   I had to sit by the hour before crackling adobe hearth or by the ruddy camp-fire, singing
each song over time after time in unison with my
good-natured instructors, until I knew the air absolutely by heart — and not only the air, but the
exact rendition of it.   To learn an air is ordinarily
simple ; but to learn a Mexican *paisano* air just as
the *paisano* sings it in New Mexico, is really a matter
of great difficulty.   By dint of perseverance, however,
I succeeded ; and at least a majority of the folk-songs
of New Mexico are at last in shape for preservation,
and none too soon, for they are fast changing and
disappearing under the new order of things.

It is curious how little the New Mexican is a
singer.   Unlike the clear-voiced Sonoran, he seems
not to have the wherewithal, though his intention is
equally tuneful.   Among the native Californians
beautiful voices are not rare ; but California is a land
where nature herself knows how to sing.   In arid,
lonely, gaunt New Mexico, where the centuries have
been so beset with danger that speech sank to timid
intonation, and where nature herself seems dumb,
music has taken the imprint of its surroundings.
The *paisano* sings in palpable doubt of his own
voice.   Perhaps that phenomenally dry atmosphere
has somewhat dessicated his larynx, too.*   At all
events, his tones are very apt to be husky.   He slurs
his notes sadly, and is prone to reduplicate them.
He sings always *con espresione*, but to him expression
has but two devices.   The more he is inspired, the

* And yet, as I have noted, the voices of the Pueblos are almost universally
clear.

higher he clambers after his pitch in falsetto and the more conscientiously nasal he becomes. And yet there is something far from contemptible in the humblest singing of these humble songs of the soil. While the fragrant cedar roars in the camp-fire and the huddled sheep sleep amid the mountain snows, it is well worth while to listen to the tattered shepherd as he beguiles the unparalleled loneliness of his lot with vague ditties of his own. And when these folk-songs are well sung, some of them are really charming. There is always one salvation. Clear-voiced or husky, the Mexican is invariably a master of time. His technique may fail at other points, but the *tempo* is faultless. It is so in his singing and in his playing. To certain simple instruments he seems to have been born. He can always play the *musica*, or harmonica, and he learns the concertina with great ease, and also the guitar. He has, too, a rude musical apology of his own, invented in and confined to the sheep camp— the *bijuela*. This is a giant jews-harp made of a bow with a key and one string. When he can afford it, this string is a guitar-gut and the bow made of hard wood and three feet long. But in case of need a *bijuela* can be constructed of a fairly stiff weed-stalk and a linen thread. One end of the bow is held between the teeth, with the string outward, and it is "fanned" in the precise manner of a jews-harp. The resultant air is more audible and not without sweetness.

The shepherd's life is the loneliest in New Mexico —if not in the world—and he is the largest producer of folk-songs. Away in the bleak wilderness for months at a time, with no other companionship than that of his two thousand maddening woolly wards, his two dogs, and his one human comrade, unlettered and undeliberative, he must have some resource or go insane. Almost the only diversion within his power is song, and to that he turns, whether qualified or not. He can neither read nor write, but he can always make verses—for Spanish is a language which cannot *help* rhyming—and though he does not know one note from another, he can always devise an air. He has a good ear and a very quick one, and a limited natural gift of improvisation. When the old songs cease to be a bulwark against the wilderness, he is not long at a loss to make new. The majority of the home-spun songs of New Mexico are from him, since no one else has so much time for composition, nor such need of self-amusement. But many songs— and some rather creditable ones—are invented by the rare good singers who are the life of winter evenings in the little hamlets, and who are spurred by their popularity to new repertories for the benefit of admiring fireside groups.

Love is the favorite motive of New Mexican folk-songs, and generally love's pangs. As one would expect who knew the history of that long-suffering land, there is a strain of sadness in the very songs. Nearly all are in a minor key. The comic is unheard-of, the witty or sarcastic is rare, though with some clever representatives. But amid the general sighs of unrequited affection there is not lacking a certain poetic touch. Even a rude philosophy is sometimes dominant, and there are many sly turns of considerable depth and adroitness.

Among the most characteristic love-songs in my collection is the best of a host of the same title,

"Angel of Love." I learned it on a lonely stage-drive of eighty miles in Western Arizona from a tuneful Mexican who had brought it from Los Corrales, N. M., where both he and the song originated. Besides other typical qualities it fairly illustrates how much more expression the average *paisano* can get into music than into words.

ANGEL DE AMOR.

TRANSCRIBED BY HENRY HOLDEN HUSS.

ANGEL DE AMOR.

Angel de amor, tu pasion no la comprendo,
   Si la comprendo, no la puedo espresar,
Voy enceler tu languido gemido,
   Allá en la tumba, par poder descansar.

Yo no siento el que me hayas querido,
   Yo no siento el que me hayas amarlo,
Solo siento el que me hayas cambiarlo *
   Con otro hombre mas inferior que yo.

Como el que tiene una musica
   Y no la sabe tocar—
Asi se queda, hay ! el hombre en este mundo
   Cuando en el mundo no se sabe espresar.

That is, as nearly as I can preserve its spirit in English:

ANGEL OF LOVE.

O Love, your passion passes understanding ;
   I understand it, yes ! but 'twill not be exprest.
I go to hide your sighing and your anguish
   There in the tomb, where only can I be at rest.

I lament not what you did me, beloved,
   I lament not that to love you did enslave me ;
Only do I lament it that you gave me
   Up for another who is less a man than I.

Ah, like him who has a harmonica
   And not the knowledge to play,
So goes the world untuned to him forever
   Who feels, but feeling has no power to say.

   * In good Spanish these rhymes should be the past participles *amado* and *cambiado.*

More typical of the depth of lovelorn despair which marks a large class of New Mexican folk-songs, and of as characteristic melody, is the favorite "Ay! Ay! Ay!" (pronounced I! I! I! an interjection equivalent to "alas!"), composed by an uneducated but intelligent man who has some facility with hard words.

AY! AY! AY!

TRANSCRIBED BY HENRY HOLDEN HUSS.

To - ma, Luisa el puñ - al   y   tras - pa - sa   Es - te pe - cho, pero
Take, Lou - i - sa, this dag - ger and plunge it   In my bos - om,   but

an - tes   pri - me - ro,   Con - sid - e - ra   que te a - mo y   te
first, I   im - plore thee,   To re - mem - ber   I love and   a-

quie - ro, ay! ay! ay! Y   por ti me di - cén in - fel - iz.   Ay!..
dore thee, ay! ay! ay! And for thee am   a   by - word of woe.   Ay!..

....   ay! ay! Que infel - iz   es   mi suer - te!   Yo - o te a - do-
....   ay! ay! How un - hap - py   my fate is!   I..........   a - dore

ro y de - seo   ser tu a - man - te Pe - ro   tu ni   si quie - ra un in-
thee, and would   be   thy lov - er, But thou   dost not   one feel - ing dis-

stan - te, ay! ay! ay! Ni un mo - men - to te a - cuer - das   de   mi.
cov - er, ay! ay! ay! Nor a mo - ment...   be - think thee of   me.

AY! AY! AY!

Toma, Luisa, el puñal y traspasa
  Este pecho, pero antes primero
    Considera que te amo y te quiero, ay! ay! ay!
  Y por ti me dicen infeliz

Coro : Ay! ay! ay! que infeliz es mi suerte,
Yo te adoro y deseo ser tu amante,
Pero tu ni siquiera un instante, ay! ay! ay!
Ni un momento te acuerdas de mi.

Las memorias de un marajitero *
Me atormentan en cada momento ;
Ay! Dios mio, no hay sufrimiento, ay! ay! ay!
Cielo santo, yo quiero morir.—*Coro.*

Clava, clava el puñal sanguinario,
Dele muerte á mi vida y honor!
Que algun dia pagarás el rigor, ay! ay! ay!
Con otro hombre que sepas amar.—*Coro.*

Bajaré silencioso á la tumba
Á buscar mi perdido sociego,
De rodillas, ingrata, te ruego, ay! ay! ay!
Que á lo menos te acuerdes de mi.—*Coro.*

Which may be translated :

Alas !

Take, Louisa, this dagger and plunge it
In my bosom ; but first I implore thee
To remember I love and adore thee, ay! ay! ay!
And for thee am a by-word for woe.

Chorus : Ay! ay! ay! how unhappy my fate is !
I adore thee and would be thy lover ;
But thou dost not one feeling discover, ay! ay! ay!
Nor for a moment bethink thee of me.

Mem'ry gives me the pangs of a martyr,
Every instant new tortures preparing—
Ah, my God ! it is pain beyond bearing, ay! ay! ay!
Holy heaven, I ask but to die.—*Chorus.*

Drive, oh drive, the red knife in my bosom,
Death to honor and life at a blow ;
For one day thou shalt pay for my woe, ay! ay! ay!
When another shall teach thee to love.—*Chorus.*

I will go to the grave uncomplaining
If it give me a peace like the old one ;
On my knees I implore thee, my cold one,
That at least thou remember me there.—*Refrain.*

* A local word ; a corruption, apparently, of *martirio*, a martyr.

A song of much humble rhetoric and passion is the extremely quaint "Suzanita"—a duet. It was taught me by one Epiphany, a tattered sixteen-year-old shepherd of San Mateo; and I have never heard it except among the people of that remote hamlet.

SUZANITA.

Transcribed by **HENRY HOLDEN HUSS.**

Con moto.

Su - zan - i - ta,   Su - zan - i - ta,   Señ - or - i - ta, man - de u-
Lit - tle Su - sie,   lit - tle Su - sie,   Lit - tle la - dy,.... call a

sted;   Fran - que - é - me   un va - so de a - gua,   Que
cup;   I'rith-ee, give me   a glass of wa - ter,   For

ya me a - bra - zo de sed.   Ni ten - go vas - o,   ni
with thirst I'm burn - ing up.   Sir, I've nei - ther cup   nor

co - pa,   Ni en que dar - le el agua á u - sted;   Pe - ro
gob - let,   Nor wherein to give wa - ter to your lip;   But I

ten - go mi bo - qui - ta,   Con el - la se la da -
have at least my mouth, here,   From that I'll give you a

ré.   A - di - os,   Su - zan - na,   Ya - di-
sip.   Good - - bye,   my Su - sie,   And good-

rit.... a tempo.   *Moderat*

os,... bon - i - ta;....   El lun - es te ven - go á
bye,.. fair girl - ie;....   On Mon-day I'm coming to

rit.................

ver,... O' el mar - tes   de mañ - a - - ni - ta.......
see you, Or on Tuesday,   bright..... and ear - ly........

SUZANITA.

EL :

Suzanita, Suzanita,
  Señorita, mande V.
Franquéeme un vaso de agua,
  Que ya me abrazo de sed.

ELLA :

Ni tengo vaso ni copa
  Ni en que darle el agua á V.
Pero tengo mi boquita—
  Con ella se la daré.

EL :

Adios, Suzana !
  Y adios bonita !
El lunes te vengo á ver,
  O' el martes de mañanita.

Her *piecito* betrays a coquetry unusual in a maiden
of Spanish blood, and his a practicality not always
characteristic of the lover. The song may be taken
to say in English :

SUSIE.

HE :

"Little Susie, little Susie,
  Little lady, call a cup ;
Prithee give me a glass of water,
  For with thirst I'm burning up."

SHE :

" Sir, I've neither cup nor goblet
  Nor wherein to put water to your lip ;
But I have at least my mouth here—
  From that I will give you a sip."

HE :

"Good-by, my Susie,
  And good-by, fair girlie.
On Monday I'm coming to see you,
  Or on Tuesday bright and early."

A radically different view of the tender passion from the average, is that taken by the cynical bard who composed "La Mentira." His identity is unknown, but he was plainly no shepherd. The song is beautiful—almost classic—Spanish verse; and no poet need have been ashamed of it. There can be little doubt that it is an imported song. The air is very characteristic.

LA MENTIRA.

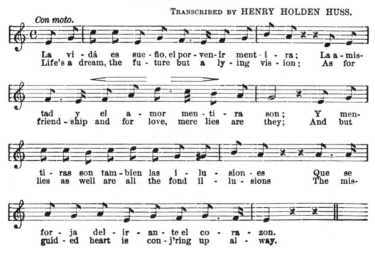

TRANSCRIBED BY HENRY HOLDEN HUSS.

Con moto.

La vi - dá es sue - ño, el por - ven - ir ment - i - ra;   La a - mis-
Life's a dream, the fu - ture but a ly - ing vis - ion;   As for

tad   y   el   a - mor men - ti - ra son ;   Y   men-
friend - ship and for love, mere lies are they;   And but

ti - ras son tam - bien las i - lu - sion - es   Que se
lies as well are all the fond il - lu - sions   The mis-

for - ja   del - ir - an - te el co - ra - zon.
guid - ed heart is con - j'ring up al - way.

LA MENTIRA.

La vida es sueño, el porvenir mentira,
  La amistad y el amor mentira son ;
Y mentiras son tambien las ilusiones
  Que se forja delirante el corazon.

Es mentira el amor de las mugeres,
Y mentira su belleza y su desden,
Y mentira el " te adoro" que pronuncian,
Y sus besos mentiras son tambien.

Son mentiras los dulces juramentos
Que pronuncian sus labios de carmin ;
Son palabras que al nacer las lleva el viento
De los prados á los bosques del confin.

Es la espina de que en vuelto va el veneno
Con que halagan su maléfico querer ;
Con que matan mestros pobres corazones—
¡ Cuan malvada, cuan malvada es la muger !

This serious arraignment, which is vastly enjoyed
in New Mexico, is by interpretation as follows :

THE LIE.

Life's a dream, the future but a lying vision,
As for friendship and for love mere lies are they;
And but lies as well are all the fond illusions
The misguided heart is conjuring-up alway.

'Tis a lie, this love the women all are feigning,
And a lie their beauty and their proud disdain,
And a lie the "I adore thee !" that they murmur,
And their very kisses are a lie as vain.

They are lies—the sweetest vows of passion
That their carmine lips breathe tenderest of all ;
They are words, and only words the winds shall scatter
Down the valley like the dead leaves of the fall.

Love ! It is the thorn that holds the hidden poison
Wherewithal they wreak their cruel whims and blind;
Wherewithal they slay our trusting hearts forever—
Ah, that wicked, ah, that wicked womankind !

Songs specifically *inter pocula* are almost unknown; but here is a semi-drinking song with love at the bottom of the cup :

EL BORRACHITO.

TRANSCRIBED BY HENRY HOLDEN HUSS.

Al bor - rach-i - to to - dó se le dis - pen - sa;
The fel - low half- seas o'er ev - 'ry one ex - cus - es;
Cuan-do an-da
When tight, he's

chis - po no con - o - ce la ver - guen - za.
not a - shamed to do just what he choos - es.
Si me em - bor -
If I get

rach - o es por u - na con - se - cuen - cia—
full, the on - ly rea - son for my booze is—
To do lo
All on ac -

cau - sa la pas - ion de un - á mu - ger.
count of pas - sion for a wom - an fair.

rit.

EL BORRACHITO.

Al borrachito todo se le dispensa,
Cuando anda chispo no conoce la verguenza ;
Si me emborracho es por una consecuencia—
  Todo lo causa la pasion de una muger.

Amigo Vino, tu me tumbas con tu aliento.
Las copas llenas onde están que no las tiento ?
Si me emborracho, es de puro sentimiento
  Porque no me ama una ingrata muger.

El whisky tomo yo por apetito—
Compro mi trago si me hace muy poquito.
Con una taza de tequila mi abuelito—
  Todo lo causa la pasion de una muger.

Or, in equivalent English :

THE DRUNKEN FELLOW.

The fellow half-seas-over everyone excuses,
When tight he's not ashamed to do just what he **chooses.**

If I get full, the only reason for my booze is
　　That my passion for a woman caused it all.

Friend Wine, your jolly, jolly breath it sends me reeling !
Where are the full cups whose red kisses I'd be stealing ?
If I get drunk, it's purely from excess of feeling,
　　Just because an ungrateful woman loves me not.

I take the whisky for the thirst that may befall one ;
I buy my drink—which seems to me a very small one,
Like my grand-dad with his glass of stuff—a tall one—
　　And a passion for a woman caused it all.

The provincial use of diminutives in New Mexico Spanish is striking, and seldom preservable in translation—unless by awkward paraphrases. Still, it always expresses a shade of meaning which is not to be lost sight of. The *borrachito*, for instance, is not *here* "the little man who is drunk," but "the man who is a little drunk." The diminutive termination serves many ends. It may be purely diminutive, as here in *apetito*, "a little appetite," or merely affectionate, as here in *abuelito*, "my little grandpa"; or even intensive as in *solito*, "*all* alone"—which in New Mexico is so much more emphatic than *solo* that a bright señorita once rebuffed me for saying I had made a certain hard journey *solito*. "What?" she cried ; "a *man* goes *solo;* but a coward thinks he is *solito*." It is hardly necessary to point out numerous other provincialisms of New Mexican Spanish—like the persistent use of *onde* for *donde*— nor the frequent ill-grammar, except in cases where the sense might be obscure to those who understand only Castilian Spanish. As for my translations, I have tried to get the exact *spirit* of the original and to make the English as good but no better verse.

One of the most popular folk-songs of New Mexico is the rollicking " Viejo," which has a tinge of humor in its words, as well as a taking swing in its measure.

EL VIEJO.

TRANSCRIBED BY HENRY HOLDEN HUSS.

To - dos di - cen que soy un vi - e - jo, Yo no
They all say I'm a worth-less old fel - low, But I

sé en que se pue - den fun - dar,... Yo me en-cuentro tan gor-do y ro-
know not by what they can score,.. For I find my-self mer-ry and

bus - to Que tres ve - ces me pue - do cas - ar, En el
mel - low, And quite fit for three mar - ri - ages more. How the

mor - ro pas - ea - ba el jo - ven, Com - ba - tien - do con-
lad held his own in the cas - tle, Fight-ing off the in-

tra el in - va - sor. Tan - to san - gre en los cam - pos re-
vad - er a - main. Blush ye not, ye in - vad - ers and

ga - ba, No te cau - sa ver - guen-za, trai - dor?
trait- ors, Thus with blood to be wat - er - ing Spain?

EL VIEJO.

Todos dicen que soy un viejo—
   Yo no sé en que se pueden fundar.
Yo me encuentro tan gordo y robusto
   Que tres veces me puedo casar.

Coro : En el morro paseaba el joven
   Combatiendo contra el invasor.
Tanto sangre en los campos regaba,
   ¿ No te causa verguenza, traidor ?

Soy un viejo de noventa años,
    Los cuento desde que empezé á andar.
Las muchachas me niegan los besos,
    Y conmigo no quieren bailar !—*Coro.*

Todos dicen ! " hipócrito viejo !"
    Paque en misa me gusta rezar,
Y en el baile me gusta tener
    Una novia á quien apretar.

In English it is difficult to render this as cleverly.

THE OLD MAN.

They all say I'm a useless old fellow,
    But I know not by what they can score ;
For I find myself merry and mellow
    And quite fit for three marriages more.

Chorus : How the lad held his own in the castle,
    Fighting off the invader amain !
Blush ye not, ye invaders and traitors,
    Thus with blood to be watering Spain ?

I am old, if it's old to be ninety—
    Ninety years since to walk I began ;
Not a kiss will the silly girls give me,
    Not a dance will they give the old man !—*Chorus.*

" You old hypocrite ! " everyone tells me,
    Just because at the ball and the mass
I am faithful alike—I love praying,
    And stepping the dance with a lass.

The refrain is evidently parasitic, for there are no castles in New Mexico. This chorus—which dates from the Moorish wars—has been borrowed from some song of the Mother Country and tacked to the "Viejo" regardless of sense. The verses and the air, however, are genuinely New Mexican, so far as I can learn.

Of the characteristic mental and musical processes of the undiluted New Mexican, there is probably no better example than that favorite oddity, the *Coyotito*—the little coyote. Its stress is fairly grotesque—as is almost the rule among these folk-songs. Hardly ever do the exigencies of the measure permit all the words to be given their proper accent. Take as a fair example the line properly pronounced :

Los cuénto désde que empiezé andár,

which is and *must* be sung

Los cuentó desde que empiezé andár.

But in the Coyotito alone do I remember the forcible splitting of a word in twain and leaving the halves parted by the impassable gulf of a full rest—as befalls in the first line of every verse of this song, and more or less in other lines. The text is sly and unusually difficult of translation, but not immoral. The ditty is very popular, and a great many postscript verses have been added ; but the apparent original will suffice here.

EL COYOTITO.

TRANSCRIBED BY HENRY HOLDEN HUSS.

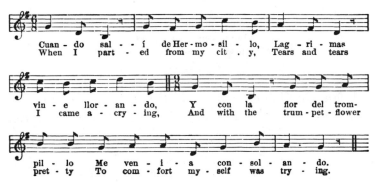

Cuan - do sal - - í de Her - mo - sil - lo, Lag - ri - mas
When I part - ed from my cit . y, Tears and tears

vin - e llor - an - do, Y con la flor del trom-
I came a - cry - ing, And with the trum - pet - flower

pil - lo Me ven - i - a con - sol - an - do.
pret - ty To com - fort my - self was try - ing.

El Coyotito.

Cuando salí de Hermosillo,*
   Lágrimas vine llorando,
Y con la flor del trompillo
   Me venia consolando.

Yo soy como el coyotito
   Que los revuelco y los dejo,
Y me voy al trotecito
   Mirando por *debajejo.*†

Ya se cayó el pino verde
   Onde habitan los pichones;
Ya cayó él que andaba ausente—
   Ahora verán pelones.

Ya se cayó el jacalito‡
   Onde colgaba mi espada.
Paque es tanto laberinto
   Si alcabo todo se acaba.

Ya se cayó el jacalito
   Onde colgaba mi espejo.
Debajo del roble encinito
   Tendió su cama un conejo.

Ya se secó el nopalito
   Onde ibamos á las tunas.
Ya me no mas anderás celando
   Con tus celos en ayunas.

Les encargo mis amigos
   Que si ven á mi querida,
No le digan que estoy preso—
   Porque es el bien di me vida.

A fair English equivalent of this remarkable ditty—
so thoroughly a folk-song in standpoint, rhetoric,

---

* A city in New Mexico.
† A diminutive for *debajo* (below).
‡ A little *jacal*, the house of chinked palisades.

rhyme, and *non sequiturs*—is perhaps unattainable.
The nearest I can come is this :

THE LITTLE COYOTE.

When I par-ted from my city,
    Tears and tears I came a-crying,
And with the trumpet-flower pretty
    To comfort myself was trying.

I am like the *coyotito*
    That just rolls them over and leaves them,
And I go trotting so neat, oh,
    My downcast glance deceives them.

Fallen is al-ready the stately
    Pine where doves perched by the air-full.
He who was gone has happened home lately,
    And the short-haired had better be careful.

Fallen is al-ready the humble
    Hut where my sword was suspended ;
What's the use of fuss and of grumble,
    If all things at last are ended ?

Fallen is al-ready the lonely
    Hut where my mirror was peeping ;
And in the oak-thickets only
    The rabbit has stretched for sleeping.

Dried is now the prickly-pear cooling
    That we both hunted when younger ;
Now me no more wilt thou go fooling
    With thy jealous tricks in my hunger.

Friends, I charge ye all unshaken,
    If my sweetheart ye be seeing,
Tell her not that I have been taken,
    For she is the good of my being.

Scarcely less characteristic in its way, but of a different phase of New Mexican life—the contact of the Saxon—is the curious folk-song of

EL FERROCARRIL.

Transcribed by HENRY HOLDEN HUSS.

Alli vi-en-e el fer-ro-car-ril,.... Va-mos á
The.... rail-road is com-ing this way,... Let us go

ver on-de 'stá.... Ah! que gus-to nos da-rá.....
look at it near... Ah! what a joy it will be,....

Cuan-do lo veá-mos ven-ir! Lle-gan-do la e-mi-gra-
When we shall see it ap-pear! And when the tour-ists shall

cion, "Good morn-ing," re-pet-i-ré, "Come in! come
throng, "Good morn-ing," I will re-peat, "Come in! come

in!" les di-ré,.... "Ven-gan o-ir mi can-cion."
in!" I'll en-treat,.. "Come ye, and list to my song."

El Ferrocarril.

Alli viene el ferrocarril,
    Vamos á ver onde 'sta.
¡ Ah, que gusto nos dará
    Cuando lo veamos venir !

Coro : Llegando la emigracion,
    " Good morning," repetiré ;
" Come in ! Come in ! " les diré,
    Vengan oir mi cancion.

De Chihuahua Franquilin *
    Corren los Americanos,
    Ganandoles el dinero
    Á todos los Mejicanos.—*Coro.*

* Franklin, the first railroad name of El Paso.

Si fueras al campamiento
    Onde vienen trabajando,
    Yo asi me vivo cantando
Para ganar el sostento.—*Coro.*

Ni el sol ni el viento podrá
    Hacerme retroceder ;
    Millas y millas correr,
Para ganar nuestro bien.—*Coro.*

La maquina va partir,
    Esten toditos alerta.
    Vayan sacando el dinero
Que ya vamos á partir.—*Coro.*

THE RAILROAD.

The railroad is coming this way—
    Let us go look at it near.
    When we shall see it appear,
Ah, what a joy it will be.

Chorus : And when the tourists shall throng,
    " Good morning ! " I will repeat ;
    " Come in ! Come in ! " I'll entreat,
" Come ye and list to my song ! "

Up from the town on the line
    Come running the *Americanos,*
    Earning us everyone money—
Money for all us *paisanos.—Chorus.*

Were you at the camp where they're giving
    Work, and the laborers bringing—
    That's just the way I live singing
Only to earn me a living.—*Chorus.*

Neither sun, neither wind shall nor could
    Make me turn back till I've done ;
    Mile after mile I will run
That I may win us some good.—*Chorus.*

The engine is going to start.
    Lively ! Be all of you ready !
    Come, pull your money out—steady,
For now we are going to start !—*Chorus.*

An attractive song which has become rooted in New Mexico, but was clearly written by a Sonoran, and perhaps in Sonora, is the "Sonoreño." It is the best Mexican version of "Home, Sweet Home," that I have found.

EL SONOREÑO.

Transcribed by HENRY HOLDEN HUSS.

EL SONOREÑO.

Virtiendo lágrimas tristes y amargas
Paso las horas en mi mente aquí;
No estoy tranquilo en los dulces zefiros
Del triste valle donde yo nací.

Coro : Solo me estorba la estruendosa música
    Que va tocando por aquí alli,
    En recordar del silencio funebre
    Del triste valle donde yo nací.

    Aquí se miran diferentes fábricas
    Y de madera que no conocí ;
    Mas no las cambio por aquellas chozas
    Del triste valle donde yo nací.—*Coro.*

    Y aquí se miran mil grupos de pájaros,
    Golillas de oro y alas de rubí ;
    Mas no las cambio por aquellas tortolas
    Del triste valle donde yo nací.—*Coro.*

    Y aquí se miran diferentes flores
    Que con su aroma luego me dormí ;
    Mas no las cambio por la flor de tuna
    Del triste valle donde yo nací.—*Coro.*

    Y aqui se ostentan las gillardas jovenes
    Tan coronadas de virtud ye allí,
    Mas no son tiernas como aquellas virgenes
    Del triste valle donde yo nací.—*Coro.*

THE SONORAN (EXILE).

With sad and bitter tears and thoughts a-wandering
    I pass the hours here with a heart forlorn ;
No more to cheer me breathe the zephyrs soft and low
    Of that poor little vale where I was born.

Chorus : It but confuses me, this din of music here,
    That blares on every street both night and morn,
And makes me miss the more the lonely, deathly hush
    Of that poor little vale where I was born.

    Ah, here I look on mansions tall and grand—
    Such homes as never my bare land adorn ;
    But for them all I would not give one hut of reeds
    In that poor little vale where I was born.—*Chorus.*

And here I look on many brilliant-feathered birds
  With throats of gold and wings as red as morn ;
But for them all I would not give the turtle-doves
  Of that poor little vale where I was born.—*Chorus.*

And here I look on many a rare and brilliant flower,
  Whose drowsy perfume makes me more forlorn ;
But for them all I would not give the cactus-flower
  Of that poor little vale where I was born.—*Chorus.*

And here are brightest, fairest damsels all to see,
  So queenly decked with all that can adorn ;
But, ah ! they are not like the tender, barefoot maids
  Of that poor little vale where I was born !—*Chorus.*

A quaint little song of the *Carbonero* purports to
have been composed in El Pino, a tiny hamlet on the
edge of the Navajo Reservation, on the verge of the
greatest coal-measures in New Mexico. But while
the ditty may have been formulated there, and even
may apply to the peasant diggers of coal, it is altogether too suggestive of Central Mexico, where the
charcoal-burner is a part of the landscape.

EL CARBONERO.

Transcribed by HENRY HOLDEN HUSS.

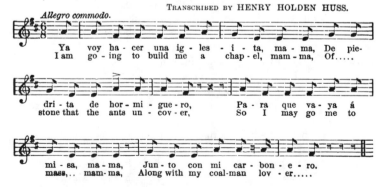

El Carbonero.

El primer amor que tengo, Mamá,
  Há de ser un carbonero.
Va á vender su carbón, Mamá,
  Pero gastando dinero.

Alli viene el carbonero, Mamá,
  Bajando por la cuchilla ;
Va á vender su carbón, Mamá,
  Á real y medio la quartilla.

Alli viene el carbonero, Mamá,
  Bajando por los corrales ;
Va sacudir su carbón, Mamá,
  Pero guardando los costales.

Ya voy hacer una iglesita, Mamá,
  De piedrita de hormiguero,
Para que vaya á misa, Mamá,
  Junto con mi carbonero.

Ya voy hacer una casita, Mamá,
  De piedrita de hormiguero,
Para vivir alli solita, Mamá,
  Junto con mi carbonero.

The Charcoal-Man.

The very first sweetheart I've had, Mamma,
  Has to work at charcoal-burning ;
He has to go selling his coals, Mamma,
  But bravely spends all he's earning.

Ah, yonder he comes, my coal-man, Mamma,
  Descending the ridge at leisure ;
He's selling the charcoal he made, Mamma,
  At a dime and a half the pint measure.

16

Ah, yonder he comes, my coal-man, Mamma,
  Coming on down by the stable ;
He's going to shake out the charcoal, Mamma,
  But saves the sacks when he's able.

I am going to build me a chapel, Mamma,
  Of pebbles the ants uncover,
So I may go me to mass, Mamma,
  Along with my coal-man lover.

I am going to build me a cottage, Mamma,
  Of pebbles the ants uncover,
So as to live there alone, Mamma,
  Along with my coal-man lover.

This is rather unusually fanciful. The *piedrita de hormiguero* means the tiny pebbles on the ant-hills, which in that locality are fragments of quartz crystals, olivines, and an occasional Navajo garnet. A chapel or cottage made of or covered with these would be indeed a fairy-tale in the land of the adobe.

Of anything like ballads, the New Mexicans have very few specimens. One of the best has its habitat in the remote hamlet of Cerros Cuates, where it is sung by two bird-voiced little girls. Their father is a jet negro to whom Spanish is the native tongue, and who does not know a word of English. He is a good singer and plays half a dozen instruments ; and his wife, a Mexican woman of some beauty, has an excellent voice. The song appears to have come from Sonora—for the *gorrion* is not a New Mexican bird—but has taken root from one end of the territory to the other. It has a dozen verses which need not be reproduced *in toto*.

LA CALANDRIA.

TRANSCRIBED BY HENRY HOLDEN HUSS.

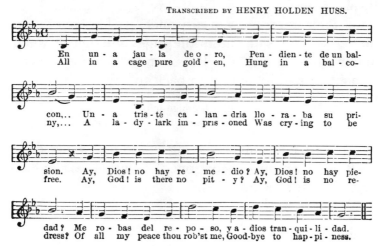

En un - a jau - la de o - ro, Pen - dien - te de un bal - con,..
All in a cage pure gold - en, Hung in a bal - co - ny,...

Un - a tris - té ca - lan - dria llo - ra - ba su pri - sion.
A la - dy - lark im - pris - oned Was cry - ing to be free.

Ay, Dios! no hay re - me - dio? Ay, Dios! no hay pie - dad?
Ay, God! is there no pit - y? Ay, God! is no re - dress?

Me ro - bas del re - po - so, y a - dios tran - qui - li - dad.
Of all my peace thou rob'st me, Good-bye to hap - pi - ness.

LA CALANDRIA.

En una jaula de oro,
   Pendiente de un balcon,
Una triste calándria
   Lloraba su prision.

Coro : ¿ Ay Dios, no hay remedio ?
    ¿ Ay Dios, no hay piedad?
   Me robas el reposo,
    Y adios tranquilidad.

Hasta un gorrioncito,
   Amoroso la hallo,
Y dijo " Mi bonita,
   Te quiero mucho yo."

Y luego la calándria
   Le dijo y le juró,
" Me sacas de mi prision,
   Me voy contigo yo."

The finch sets to work with wings and beak, and
soon breaks the wires, whereupon the ungrateful lark

flies off. He pursues and overtakes her, but she turns upon him with, "Upon my faith I never knew you, and never was a prisoner." The poor finch flies back very sad, enters the cage, and there "weeps and weeps and weeps. But soon the lark repents her treachery, and humbly flies back to say

> " No llores, amigo mio—
> Lo que pasó voló,"

which is equivalent to saying, "Do not weep, dear; we'll let bygones be bygones"—with the maidenly hint that she is now his.

THE CALENDAR-LARK.

All in a cage pure golden,
  Hung in a balcony,
A lady-lark imprisoned
  Was crying to be free.

Chorus : Ay, God ! is there no pity ?
    Ay, God ! is no redress ?
  Of all my peace thou robst me,
    Good-by to happiness.

Until a young finch-gallant
  By chance a-passing flew
And said, " My little beauty,
  I love you much, I do ! "—*Chorus.*

And straightway then the larkling,
  She promised fair and true:
"Oh, take me from my prison,
  And I will go with you ! "

A very different ballad equally of folk-song rank, but much more clever in motive and treatment, is a New Mexican version of " Venus and Adonis." Venus is much less ornate but much more modest than

Shakespeare's; and Adonis a less rhetorical and more human clown, in that he repents at the eleventh hour.

EL PASTOR TONTO.

TRANSCRIBED BY HENRY HOLDEN HUSS.

Un - a niña en un bal - con... Le di - - - ce á
In a bal - co - ny a dam-sel Cried out, Oh, stay,

un pas-tor, "Es - pe - ra! Que a - qui te ha - bla un-a pa-
to a shep-herd star-ing, For... here a ten - der dove be-

lo - ma, Que de a - mor,...... se des - - es-
speaks you, Who is for love...... and you de-

pe - ra." "No me ha-blas de esa ma - ne - ra,"
spair - ing." "Oh, you mustn't speak to me in that way,"

re - spon - di - ó el vil - lan - o vil, "Mi ga-
Re - plied... the dull and stu - pid clown, "For my

nad - o 'sta en la sier - ra. Con él me hé de ir á dor-mir"
flock is in the mountains, With it I must go lay me down,"

EL PASTOR TONTO.

Una niña en un balcon
  Le dice á un pastor " Espera,
Que aqui te habla una paloma ⎫
  Que de amor se desespera." ⎬ *Bis.*

" No me hables de esa manera,"
  Respondió el villano vil;
" Mi ganado 'sta en la sierra, ⎫
  Con él me hé de ir á dormir." ⎬ *Bis.*

" Oyes, pastor tan hermoso,
  Que aqui te habla una paloma.
Arrimate por acá
  Ni haya miedo que te coma." } *Bis.*

" Bien estás San Pedro en Roma,"
  Respondió el villano vil,
" Mi ganado 'stá en la sierra,
  Con él me hé de ir á dormir." } *Bis.*

Then follow half a dozen verses of allurements, the " paloma " offering successively a pile of gold, three vases of perfume, a flock of burros, and at last her own beautiful hair as a bribe to the *paisano* excelsior to " pause." But in each case he answers " Tu no me enredas con ellos "—" You will not trap me with those "— and reiterates his intention of passing the night with that precious flock. In the next to the last verse, however, he suddenly sees a great light, and for the first time gets through his skull that love and not nonsense is calling. He apologizes to the " *gran señora*," and trusts he has not offended. But, not altogether unwomanlike, she has no more patience for such a stupid winning, and turns him off with a couplet which is as gratifying to the reader's sense of justice as it must have been to her pride:

" Cuando quise, no quisistes,
  Y ahora que quieres no quiero."

" When I would, thou wouldst not ;
  And now when thou wouldst, I will **not.**"

THE STUPID SHEPHERD.

In a balcony a pretty damsel
  Cried out, " Oh, stay !" to a shepherd **staring,**
" For here a tender dove bespeaks you
  Who is for love and you despairing." } *Bis.*

" Oh, you mustn't speak to me in that way ! "
  Replied the dull and stupid clown ;
" For my flock is in the mountains,
  With it I have to go and lay me down." } *Bis.*

" Listen, shepherd, tall and handsome,
  For here a tender dove doth greet you ;
Come nigh, and don't be acting
  As if afraid that I might eat you." } *Bis.*

" I wouldn't care 'f you were St. Peter
  In Rome," replied the foolish clown ;
" For my flock is in the mountains,
  And there I must go lay me down." } *Bis.*

It is not surprising that amid the folk-songs of New Mexico are none descriptive of the life led by so large a proportion of the men—that of the shepherd—and none more closely alluding to it than the *Pastor Tonto.* Its realities are ever present, and the singer is glad enough to forget them, at least while he sings, and turn to more alluring subjects. But one would expect to find songs relative to the saddle—in which most New Mexicans are proficient—the guitar, the dance, and, above all, the cigarette. Everyone smokes ; and yet I think it is safe to say that there is not one indigenous folk-song in the Southwest about the soothing *cigarro.* There is one Spanish song placing the weed above love and other luxuries, which may now be heard in hundreds of New Mexican homes throughout the territory. But lest any later student in the field be deceived by coming across this song, it is fair to say that I wrote it myself in 1889, to please my *paisano* friends in return for their patience in teaching me real songs of the soil, and that it has been welcomed and adopted into their repertories.

Besides the folk-songs, of which I have tried to give a fair idea by these types from among thousands, there are vast quantities of *dichos*, or epigrammatic verses, proverbial rhymes, and the like. Nearly everyone at some time has made a *dicho;* and the fittest survive. Of the simplest form are such verses as:

> Mucho me gusta el queso,*
>   El queso de mi rancho.
> Mas me gusta un beso
>   De los del sombrero ancho.

> Much I fancy cheese like this—
>   The cheese from my rancho fat.
> But more I fancy a stolen kiss
>   From those of the broad-brimmed hat.

Or this:

> Ojos amables,
>   Color de café,
> Deme un beso
>   De buena fé.

> Lovable eyes
>   Of coffee hue,
> Give me a kiss
>   Of faith all true.

Of the more epigrammatic form one popular *dicho* will suffice:

> Las negras son de oro,
>   Las trigueñas son de plata,
> Las gueras no mas de cobre,
>   Y las blancas de oja de lata.

> Dark women are good as gold ;
>   Brunettes like silver win ;
> The blondes are only copper,
>   And the light ones only tin.

* This seems to have been taken from a Sonoran folk-song, *"La Gorra."*

Another version says * :

> Las Morenas hiso Dios,
>   Á las blancas un platero,
> Las trigueñas hiso un sastre
>   Y á las negras un zapatero.

> God made the swarthy women ;
>   A silversmith the white ones ;
> The dark brunettes, a tailor ;
>   A cobbler the black-as-night ones.

As an example of the moral philosophy of the maker of *dichos*, we may take the following :

> No hay mas amigo que Dios,
>   Esto es claro y evidente ;
> Que el mas amigo es traidor,
>   Y el mas verdadero miente.

> There is no better friend than God,
>   This is clear and past denying ;
> For the dearest may betray,
>   The most truthful may be lying.

A disquieting thought, which has found expression in many languages, marks this popular *dicho :*

> Boquita de coral fino,
>   Labios de azucar inglés,
> Boquita de piloncillo—
>   ¿ Quien te besará otra vez?

> Little mouth of coral fine,
>   Lips of store-bought sugar, this you
> Make me wonder, little mouth—
>   Who will be the next to kiss you?

* In these songs I have frequently used accents to indicate the stress which requires many words to be sung with an entirely wrong accent.

A decidedly dainty fancy, though clad in homespun, is this :

> Suspiros que de aquí salen,
>   Y otros que de allá vendrán,
> Si en el camino se encuentran,
>   Que de cosas no se dirán.
>
> My sighs, that go and leave me here,
>   And yours from yonder stealing out—
> If on the road they chance to meet,
>   How many things they'll talk about !

X

A DAY OF THE SAINTS

A DAY OF THE SAINTS

THERE is hardly to be seen within the range of practicable travel a sight more picturesque or more stirring than that of a saint's day in a Pueblo town. Each pueblo has its patron saint in the Catholic Church, to whose honor the appropriate day of the calendar is set apart; and with the unhypocritical duplicity of these quaint folk it is always contrived to do homage to the *santo* and to all the pagan Trues at one fell swoop. The *cachinas* or sacred dances which were in vogue before Columbus, still survive; but now they are applied to the festivals of the church, and are presumed to be as grateful to *Tata Dios* as to the Sun-Father and the Hero Twins. That is, the unobjectionable ones. There were many which had to be sternly suppressed; for the aboriginal theology, with its corner-stone of sex, had many features which could hardly be brought to church. They were not vile, for they were sincerely religious, but under our different standards of what may and what may not be paraded, they would seem highly indecorous.

But of entirely "proper" *cachinas* enough remain to furnish forth appropriately every saint's day in the long calendar. Of such a fiesta, the dance of the Ayash-tyúcotz in Cochití is a fair type. I shall speak of it here only from its popularly visible side, without attempting to present its scientific significance and details.

The great feast of San Buena Ventura de Cochití —the full name of the pueblo whose known wanderings have already been traced—falls on July 14th, the calendar day of its patron San Buena Ventura.

Cochití, as it is ordinarily called for short, lies on the gravel mesa on the west bank of the Rio Grande, twenty-five miles southwest of Santa Fé. It is one of the smallest of the pueblos, and one of the least striking ; but it gets up a dance that would do no discredit to any of them. It belongs to the Quéres group of pueblos, in which are also included the towns of Santa Ana, San Felipe, Santo Domingo, Acoma, Zia, and Laguna. These seven speak the same language ; while all around are others whose tongues are radically different. In the old mission days the population of Cochití was 656, but to-day it must be a scant 200. It has plenty of fine farming land, well cultivated, and is well-to-do in the matter of herds and grazing lands.

Driving down over the hot plains from Santa Fé, bumping down the hideous La Bajada—a great lava hill, almost a precipice—one comes at length to the jumping-off place of the river mesas, and looks upon the lovely valley of the Rio Grande. It would be a beautiful sight anywhere ; and doubly beautiful it is in this bare, brown country, whose broad bosom shows the stranger little of its fertile possibilities. On the west the broken mass of the noble Valles range climbs the sky, and from a gap in its foothills issues the silver ribbon of the finest river in New

A DAY OF THE SAINTS, ACOMA.—THE PROCESSION.

Mexico. Between scalloped mesas it winds its way to the south in a broad belt of green, patched numerously with the waving yellow of ripe wheat and dotted with noble trees as those that grace the intervales of the Connecticut.

At our feet the quaint little Mexican plaza of Peña Blanca nestles amid its huge cottonwoods; and across the rippling river the morning sun shines bright upon the front of the mission church of Cochití, whitewashed for the occasion, and upon the scattered brown adobes of the town.

Early on the morning of the feast—" early " in a Mexican town means 9 A.M.—heavy farm wagons, loaded to the muzzle with *paisanos*, begin to rumble along the one straggling street of Peña Blanca, headed Cochitíward. The men driving are in black suits and shirt-sleeves; the female contingent, seated in the wagon-bed upon straw, are in spotless and flappy white, and shaded as to their faces by more or less kaleidoscopic hats and parasols. A New Mexican girl, who is pretty at home in the simple dignity of a single calico dress, is a sight for gods and men when arrayed for a *fiesta*. The fit of her dress is fairly epileptic.

Joining the intermittent procession, we dare the ticklish ford—the Rio Grande is always a treacherous river to cross—and are soon climbing from the fertile bottom to the low gravel bench upon which the rather rambling town is built.

A little above the ford, and hidden from its publicity by a bend in the river, is a quiet pool whither the women repair with their water-jars and babes; and here this morning is a picture as Arcadian as shall well be found. There is no more modest people than this ; but children hardly "count," and the bare-breeked tots are everywhere, crowing and bedimpled. Here at the watering pool, youngsters from three to twelve doff their simple garments and tumble into the river, boys and girls together, and romp and swim and splash in infinite innocent mirth. Perfect little ducks they are, apparently as much at home in the water as ashore. Mothers hold four-months-old babes off shore, chin-deep in the eddies ; and the fat brownies chuckle and squeal with glee. Maidens of sixteen, comely of face and superb in figure, throw off their head-shawls and heavy *mantas*, unwind their buckskin "boots," and in the clinging *camisa* plunge in with girlish shrieks. Staid matrons do likewise, or wade out knee-deep and stand there washing their skirts. Here the Milonian Venus might find a dozen sisters—such noble forms as were before the monstrosity of "civilized" dress.

There is not a suggestive word or motion—all is the simplicity of Eden before the snake. And when they have swum and splashed and frolicked to their hearts' content, the comely bathers run ashore and don the discarded garments, and poise the brimming water-jars on confident heads, and march up the steep path homeward, while new relays come to take their places.

All is gay in the pueblo. Bustle is a word which hardly applies to anything New Mexican, but everyone is moving in that sedate and leisurely fashion which is *el costumbre del pais*. Now and then a Mexican visitor goes galloping break-neckfully about the town, but the Pueblos are gathered in gay-colored groups around the houses, or sauntering soberly across the open spaces. Pueblos from Santo Domingo, San Felipe, Isleta, San Juan, Nambé, Tesuque, Pojoaque, and even distant Acoma; Navajos from the western end of the Territory, half a dozen "Americans," and forty or fifty neighboring Mexicans are among the crowd.

A sudden burst of putative music and a general rush of horse and foot, call us to a little level place in front of the quaint balconied church. The whole population is there, and all the visitors. Two hundred mounted Pueblos, aligned as perfectly as a crack cavalry regiment on parade, form three sides of a hollow square. The fourth side is the high wall of the old churchyard, now buried under a drift of expectant humanity. Close by the cross over the gate are the long, faded robe and the beautiful, classic face of the priest from Peña Blanca, whose delicately chiselled Gallic features look anachronistic enough among those swarthy proselytes. He has held morning mass in the old church, and now the first dance of the day is to be *el baile del padre*, in his honor.

There is not long to wait. Directly the pum! pum! pum! of a huge yellow *tombé*, big as a mature beer-barrel, sounds around the corner of the church, presently followed by the *tombé* itself and its athletic persecutor. Around the drummer cluster the chorus—a dozen men in snowy shirts and with snowy drawers descending into the embrace of beautiful brown buckskin leggins which also cover the tops of their moccasins. They chant loudly a weird refrain in the Quéres tongue, keeping perfect time with feet and arms. They are closely followed by the dancers—a

strange and grotesque half hundred, truly.   At their
head marches the bearer of the holy Flag of the Sun.
He is a stalwart aborigine clothed upon with all pomp
and circumstance.   The banner is a priceless bit of
work in beaded buckskin, bearing, with its pole, the
general shape of a gigantic feather, and fringed and
tufted at sides and top with eagle feathers.   The
dancers are equally divided as to sex, and an attractive set in face and form.   The women wear their
usual modest dress to the knees, but have omitted
their every-day buckskin boots and moccasins, and
their shapely shins and arms are bare.   Their beautiful black hair, carefully combed, hangs down their
backs, unrestrained by ribbon or ornament.   Around
their necks they wear a dazzling profusion of necklaces.   Costly corals, silver beads alternating with
silver crosses, and long strings of priceless turquoise,
are a dozen strands deep on those pretty brown
necks.   Their heavy jet bangs wave as they come
hopping along on alternate feet.   Each has a bright
vermilion patch on either cheek-bone, and each holds
in either hand a sprig of sacred cedar.   But the most
remarkable feature of the female garb is the head-
dress.   Over the middle of her crown each woman
wears a board, fitted to her head, and rising eighteen
inches above it.   This board is bright green, with an
ornamental top and a capital T sawed out of the
middle.   The projections at the top of the board are
prettily tufted.   The women are all young and comely, and extremely modest in demeanor—as Pueblo
women always are.

The men are more picturesquely arrayed.   Each
is naked to the waist, and painted over the trunk and

DANCE OF THE AYASH-TYÚ-COTZ.

arms with a dull blue.   Around the waist and falling
nearly to the knees, is an elaborate dancing-skirt
woven of mouse-colored stuff, handsomely decked
with bead work, and with a curious corded sash pendent on the right side.   To this skirt, behind, is attached a beautiful fox skin, with its long brush dangling nearly to the ground.   The moccasins and leggins complete the dress, but there are further accessories.   Each man has fastened to the top of his head
a little bunch of feathers or a sprig of cedar ;   each has
around his biceps a four-inch armlet of buckskin
painted green and white, and several skeins of bright
yarn and strings of sleigh-bells are tied around the
leggins just below the knee.   None of them wear face
paint, none have the customary headkerchief or cue,
nor the every-day white cotton drawers.   Each holds
in his left hand a branch of evergreen, and in his right
a rattle made of a dry gourd, with a wooden handle.
Over their bare chests rattle beads only less prodigal
than those worn by the women.   The men are all
young or youngish and, as a rule, very good-looking
fellows.   At the rear the procession tapers down to
half a dozen boys and girls, the smallest not over four
years old, but dressed just like their elders, and equally
expert in the intricacies of the curious dance.

When the fifty dancers are all inside the square, in
a long row by pairs—first two women and then two
men—they cease their advance, which has been made
at a madding pace of a half a mile per hour, but continue to "mark time," to the unfaltering bump of the
yellow drum and the long-winded sing-song of the
chorus.   The step, whether advancing, retreating, or
standing still, is the same—a simple variation of the

universal hop-jump remembered by everyone who has ever seen an aboriginal dance. Starting on tiptoe, the dancer raises his right foot quickly to a height of from three to six inches above the ground, at the same time—or perhaps an instant later—giving a tiny hop, which lifts the left foot high enough to put a toothpick between it and the ground. This hitch is almost imperceptible in itself, but it is never omitted, and makes a notable impression upon the character of the step as a whole. Then the right foot goes down in a similar hyphenated fashion, and the left foot up, and so on. The soft pat of the moccasined feet of the men and the bare soles of the women are audible only in the aggregate.

After a little marching and countermarching around the space reserved for them, the dancers again come down to the footlights—so to speak —and, by a quick turn, form in four parallel rows, facing outward. In the centre are the two rows of women, and on each side a row of men. In this position they dance in mark-time fashion, moving their arms up and down alternately with their legs. The men use their rattles meantime, each at stated intervals thrusting his right arm out sharply from the shoulder and giving at the same time a loud " Ay! ay ! " All sway their bodies from side to side, also, in graceful wise. The time kept by all is absolutely faultless, and the figures remind one of a Virginia reel. Up and down between the open lines of the dancers gambol the *entremiseros* or *kó-sha-re*, three tall, erect fellows, who are the most important characters of the day. They are naked save for their G-string and various charmed knots bound about knees and arms ; and covered from toe to topknot with a film of *yeso*—a bluish-white clay. Upon this light ground are drawn zigzag lightnings and other figures in black. The eyes are surrounded by four-inch "spectacles" of paint. Their long hair is drawn into a thick wad over each ear, standing out horizontally; while an equal wisp of shredded corn-husks, woven at right angles, bristles on the perpendicular. Other wisps of corn-husk are bound to their ankles, along with dangling shells of the sacred tortoise and bony sheep-trotters. These are the official clowns—the potent Delight-Makers; and many a note of approbation is called out by their fantastic monkey-shines.

After this sort of thing has gone on for half an hour, the standard-bearer gives the word, the *tombé* receives an accelerated drubbing and the squad of dancers, doubling on itself, dances inchingly out of the square and disappears around the corner of the church. At once a new *tombé*—this time a gay green one—asserts itself; and in a moment more another half hundred dancers are filing in, headed by the self-same drum-major and pranced about by the self-same *entremiseros*. The only difference between this squad and the first is that the women's head-dresses in this are arched at the top, while in the first they were serrate. The newcomers dance half an hour and then make way again for their predecessors.

After the first company has finished its second dance the drum gives another rattle, and the crowd breaks for the plaza, or public square, followed by the deliberate dancers. This square is some two hundred feet on a side, shut in by the quaint adobe houses, and with alleys running out at each corner.

The space enclosed slopes gently to the centre, where
a pool of rain-water, some forty feet in diameter, has
formed from a summer shower. Against a preten-
tious and somewhat Mexicanized house on the south
side of the plaza is built a big, rude booth of cedar ;
and in this, guarded by two small boys with venerable muskets, presides the gracious lady of the day,
San Buena Ventura, in paint and plaster. She stands
on a rough hand-barrow, on whose handles numerous
candles flare in the rising wind. Close by this outdoor shrine are the fakirs of the day—two Mexicans
with a tub of alleged lemonade, and a Santo Domingo
Indian with a big box of apricots the size and flavor
of a musty dried prune. Neither of them do much
business, except with the visiting Mexicans. The
natives have dry-prune apricots of their own, which
they munch with white teeth and an air of content-
ment ; and very few of them are caught by the
lemonade swindle.

Upon every housetop around the square are picturesque groups in all the gayety of color and lavish-
ness of ornament peculiar to this strange race. Cochití is a flat pueblo. It has very few two-storied
(terraced) houses, and is almost entirely composed of
one-storied adobes—in marked contrast to the finer
pueblos. But whether two stories or only one, the roofs
are all well occupied now. Along the north side of
the plaza are gathered most of the horsemen who had
watched the former dance. The most striking thing
about the group to one familiar with this country is
the wonderful display of fine Navajo blankets. Cheap
blankets of that make are common enough, but fine
ones are becoming very rare. There are twenty-five

here worth $50 apiece, forty worth $25 apiece, and thirty-five averaging $15 apiece. Here, then, are one hundred Pueblos whose blankets alone are worth nearly $3,000, not to mention their fine horses, their bridles buried in solid silver, and their scores of pounds of silver, coral, and turquoise ornaments.

The dancing is still done by relays, only one of the two companies occupying the plaza at the same time. With the same hair-breadth step the performers keep inching round and round the central pool ; and when they are tired, inch out by the northeast alley, while their relief inches in by the southeast—to which the relieved soon march around (outside the houses) and wait for their turn to come again.

But while the dancers are going through the same programme, the *entremiseros* are having a deal more fun. The new-formed puddle is a special dispensation in their behalf. The first one to " take a tumble " (slangily, but literally speaking) is the tallest of them, a fine sinewy specimen of manhood, whose talents as a clown would give him a good engagement with any wide-awake circus. Calling attention to himself by a wild " eyoop! " and some grotesque capers, he rushes into the middle of the pool, whirls around and throws himself full length into the water, face down. As his garb is the *reductio ad absurdum*, and the mercury aspires, he is doubtless very comfortable. His wrigglings, contortions, and antics in that puddle keep every one on a grin except the dancers ; and they would not laugh for the world. The preternatural solemnity of their faces never leaves them for an instant during the day. He lies on his back awhile, and then flops over upon his face ;

then he gets up and ambles around with an inimitable
stage trot; then he pretends to stub his toe, and falls
with the easy all-overness affected by the padded
roller-skate caricature so dear to the heart of the cir-
cus-going small boy; then he kneels and keeps ducking his face into the water, his wet hair and its bristling appendage flapping back and forth in ludicrous
harmony. Finally one of the other Delight-Makers—
the third having retired—declines to miss the fun any
longer, and he, too, tumbles into the pool. Then the
sport is doubled. Such a laughable battle—a queer
mixture of clownishness and childishness—as ensues!
Number one grapples with number two, and, after a
fierce wrestle, downs and sits upon him. They roll
each other over, splash water in each other's face,
and make the most comical exhibitions conceivable.
Finally number one wearies and retires to the dry
land. Number two sneaks up behind him until they
are back to back, and then, reaching over, grabs him,
and, taking him out to the middle of the pool on his
own back, flops him over his head into the pool—the
preface to another horse-play contest. Number two
then goes off to shake his gory locks around the
dancers for a while. Number one, after disporting
himself in the pool a bit longer, sallies out to the
shrine; and, catching up on his back a prominent
(aboriginal) citizen, who is dressed in new and blame-
less white, starts off with him at a gallop for the pool.
At its edge he is met by the returned number two,
who throws a handful of powdered blue clay all over
his wet face. Number one drops his recalcitrant burden and begins groping and stepping high in grotesque feint of blindness. The dirt-slinger squats

quietly in the middle of the pool, and watches these gropings with a funny leer. Presently number one, in his high stepping, plants his foot on the crown of number two's head, lifts himself to full height upon it, and goes sprawling headlong on the other side. At this arises as near a " roar " of laughter as you will ever hear in a Pueblo town. Number two now lies prone in the water, his head only a little lifted. Number one elevates himself and returns to the charge. Again he makes his partner's head a stepping-stone ; again the head is soused down into the water, and again number one goes headlong himself. For a dozen times or more this is repeated ; and each time it evokes as appreciative a laugh from the audience as at the outset. And so their rude play runs on until both bands of dancers are hip-hopping together in the plaza, when the services of the mirth-makers are needed. For two hours a furious sand-storm has been sweeping down the valley, nearly blinding everybody but the performers. The dance would be kept up till sunset, but at three o'clock it begins to rain emphatically, and though eyes are no object, all that feast-day finery is, and the dance ends in short order.

Meanwhile there have been exciting doings on the gravel bench back of the pueblo. The Mexican visitors have procured an ancient fowl or so and have been running their wild *gallo* race—burying the bird in the sand to the neck, to be plucked up by daring riders as they thunder past at full gallop.

A somewhat similar fight for a hog also takes place in the valley along the river, where five Pueblos, stripped to the G-string, wrestle and run for their porcine prize for a solid hour. One of them drags the hog—a razor-backed brute of no mean capacity as a racer himself—into a deep pool, and there defends him gallantly. There is a very spirited ducking match before one athletic young man finally escapes with the hog to his own house.

All day long three comfortable houses have kept their tables spread with simple food, and all who wish go there and eat, without money and without price.

All day long, too, good San Buena Ventura has been liberally attended. Solemn groups of men, women, and children have been walking soberly to her booth and leaving her the richer for their visits. The women carry flaring Apache baskets upon their heads, heaped with wheat, apricots, apples, plums, corn, melons, and the like. The dingy yellow cloth which serves the saint as a supplementary lap, sags heavier and heavier, as the hours go by, with store of votive offerings. Mothers hold up dimpled babes to kiss the holy draperies and drop a treasured nickel.

But now the house of the Sun-Father is sinking behind the peaks of Jemez. The Indian visitors are loping off homeward ; the Cochiteños seek the shelter of their adobe homes, and the Caucasians are already splashing across the ford to hold a *baile* in a clay-floored corridor under the spreading trees of Peña Blanca.

Another side of the saint's-day is seen in the *fiesta* of San Juan in Acoma. June 24th, St. John's Day, is not the most important feast of the year by any

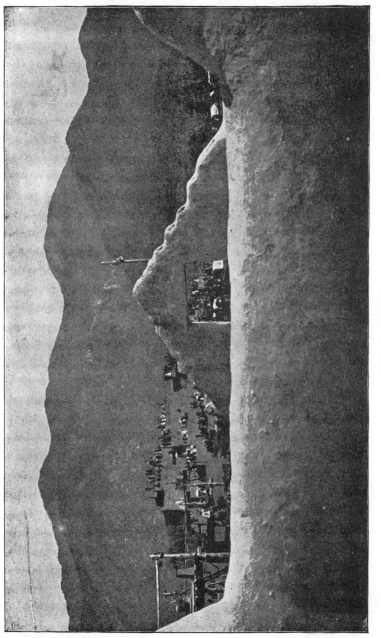

TAOS ON A FEAST-DAY.

means, being surpassed in aboriginal value by the
day of San José the pueblo's patron, and by the harvest feast; but it is the most interesting to outsiders.

When first the gray sky in the east turns to opal
on San Juan's morning all Acoma is awake. Warmer
grow the shifting tints, and at last the blood-red disk
floats above the stunted piñons of the eastern valley
wall. Upon the tops of their high, terraced houses
the children of the Sun stand motionless and rever-
ent: swathed in gorgeous blankets, bedecked with
lavish silver and coral, their buckskin *calzones* bound
with generous amplitude of brilliant garter, their long,
soft hair restrained by silken kerchiefs or bound behind in Egyptian queues, their fine figures statuesque
as a Grecian marble, their keen eyes full upon that
blinding orb in whose fatherhood they may well be
pardoned for believing. Five minutes later the motionless groups are broken up. From a hundred tall
adobe chimneys, crowned with inverted earthen pots,
the sleepy morning smoke curls skyward. Here and
there a rainbow-blanketed form glides noiselessly
along the solid rock of the lop-sided streets; and out
by the great rock cistern beyond the noble church
may be seen coming the stately line of maids and matrons marching homeward, each with a bright-hued
tinaja full of water poised gracefully upon her shawled
head, while below her quaint high boots of white
buckskin shimmer in the level sun.

At eight o'clock the streets are alive. Strong-
faced, athletic men, modest and comely women, children invariably fat and good-natured, in the easy
freedom of a single garment, the infants slung in the
bight of shawls on the backs of girls of five to ten

18

years—these are at every corner.   Up and down the
tall ladders which serve as doorsteps paddle the
chuckling children and an occasional blear-eyed dog.
Everybody is in high feather and festal dress.   The
high, sweet voices of the women twitter above the
deeper chest-tones of the men.

Presently rises a vast clatter along the *mesa's*
rocky floor, and around the corner of the church
sweeps the Acoma *caballada*—a thousand brave
ponies, lineal descendants of that Arab blood brought
here more than three centuries ago by the Spanish
cavaliers.   Behind them rides the lone Pueblo who
has rounded them up on the plain below and driven
them up the rocky staircase, built with infinite labor
a generation ago, after the patient people had tired
of the dizzy stone ladder—inaccessible to horse or
cow, or even to the sure-footed goat—which had
hitherto been their sole adit.   Wheeling through a
gap in the southernmost row of houses, the horses
halt of their own accord in the wide space between
that row and the next, and there stand in reflective
quiet, save when some irredeemable bronco turns his
heels loose at the nose of an over-inquisitive brother.

Shortly after eleven o'clock the querulous church-
bells begin to jangle in their lofty tower, and a little
procession, mostly of women, plods sedately to the
church.   Before the quaint old altar, with its rude
wood paintings and comical fluted columns, burn a
hundred candles, whose wavering flame flares upon
the ancient timbers and herring-bone ceiling of the
lofty roof.   At the head of the procession marches
the withered old native sacristan, Lorenzo Arragon—
followed by five old men singing the *misa* after a di-

A PUEBLO CHURCH AT LAGUNA.

lapidated fashion. The women bear on their heads baskets of rushes heaped high with symbolic articles. The baskets are lined with soft, green moss. Upon this dainty sward are scores of clever clay imitations of horses, steers, cows, sheep, and goats; and in front of each gayly painted *animalito* are little heaps of corn and wheat and grass. With great manœuvrings the party comes before the ancient and dilapidated wooden statue of St. John, who to-day occupies the post of honor. His multiplicative blessing is invoked that there may be great increase this year of all the property represented in the symbolic baskets; holy water is then sprinkled upon the articles, and the postulants leave the church, each to hide the sancti‐ fied basket in a secret corner of her house, there to be kept a year from date.

A little after noon the leisurely crowd begins to drift slowly over to the north street, the narrowest but smoothest of all. Where a cross street comes in, a half hundred of the leading old men of the pueblo squat upon the rocks, while around hang clusters of children. The surrounding housetops are a perfect kaleidoscope of gorgeous color and gleaming silver. The solemn-faced alguazil, with a gay green drum of rawhide slung at his side, glances around him search‐ ingly and begins to belabor the protesting instrument with two aldermanic drumsticks. Directly a group of boys of six to fifteen years begin to wriggle out of their print shirts and flapping cotton drawers. Two fat and dimpled little chubs reduce themselves to *puro pelote*. All then coat themselves with a film of white clay from a big tinaja. A few striplings of eighteen also shed their upper garments, retaining only their drawers. Then the smaller youngsters repair to the upper end of the street and stand there in a nude huddle. The drummer gives a vicious thump upon his drumhead and calls out a disjointed order. Two boys spring from the group and come flying down the street, lithe and agile as young antelopes. The smaller is bent on winning. His long black hair floats behind ; his big dark eyes shine like stars, and his chubby legs fairly twinkle along the gray rocky floor. The larger boy runs to win, too, but he is more infirm of purpose. The housetop crowds catch his eyes and the encouraging shouts of the men tickle him. He leads easily to within thirty yards of the winning-post, and then in a beautiful spurt the little fellow fairly sails to the fore and wins by a yard, amid loud applause.

Before the breathless boys can sink upon a little bed of soft, white sand, the drummer has yelled again, and another pair of biped meteors come flashing down the track. And so it goes till each couple of the fifty boys has run the two-hundred-yard course twice.

Meantime two very important looking fellows with the soberest faces in the world have brought forth two slender, strong poles of about eighteen feet in length, and tied to each near the top the end of a twenty-foot horse-hair reata. One of them then produces a loudly objecting rooster, ties his feet together with a buckskin thong, and fastens the thong to a loop in the middle of the pendent rope. Each standard-bearer then grasps his pole and draws it toward him till the intervening "lariat" is half taut. The unfortunate rooster thus dangles headlong at a height of about ten feet from the ground. The previous racers now fall into line a little way down the street, the tiniest of them in the lead. A crowd of grown-up boys and men drop in behind in the order of their altitude.

Rousing his drum from its sleepy grunting to a hoarse rattle, the alguazil shouts the signal for the sport to begin. In mechanical unanimity the long procession—there are in it one hundred and nine persons, ranging in height from six feet two inches in the rear to two feet six inches in front—with the peculiar hop-stamp, hop-stamp, moves forward with deliberate precision, passing between the poles and under the chicken in single file. Each runner has a little branch of *chaparo*, and as each passes under the flapping chanticleer he leaps high in air with a clear treble "*eeyoop!*" and a simultaneous wild swipe with his stick at the rooster, which by able ducking evades most of these offers. Passing up the street a couple of hundred yards the procession halts, doubles upon itself in a serpentine loop and starts back toward the poles at a notably accelerated pace. This time each runner jumps higher, strikes harder, and "eeyoops" louder, and the worried target has to double its agility to clear the flying switches. Up and down, down and up, the procession runs half a score of times in physical and vocal crescendo. On the last stretch each runner hurls his light switch at the mark.

Still in line, the runners now rest a moment. The pole-holders step each a step inward, so that the rooster hangs several feet nearer the ground. Again the drummer signals, and again the running begins.

Now each runner makes a frantic leap and clutch for the prize, the pole men at the same instant twitching the poles outward so that the rooster bobs high above the reach of the jumper. In this fashion the procession prances back and forth eight or ten times. Suddenly a tall, finely built fellow makes a superhuman lunge into the air and catches the rooster by the neck before the guards can swing it aloft. With a single powerful thrust of his arm he bursts the buckskin thong, and with a wild yell breaks from the line and is off like a deer, swinging the astounded bird triumphantly above his head. The whole pack is at his heels in an instant, and amid the excited shrieks of the spectators, the chase sweeps down the street and around the corner of the houses. Round and round the block they run, the pursued doubling and turning like a jackrabbit to elude the wild grabs of his pursuers. When at last the tremendous pace begins to tell even on his deep lungs, he whirls and brings the chicken down with a resounding thump upon the bare shoulders of the foremost of the field. The youth thus challenged seizes the trophy and flies ahead with it, the crowd following him as before. Those who are shorter of wind—in every case the " educated " boys—lie off in corners and resume the chase when it comes around again. For nearly half an hour this remarkable running continues at a five-minute gait or less, the rooster changing hands five times meanwhile. Then the runners come to a dead stop in the wide spot in front of the open place, and the one who holds the rooster, turning to the nearest of his companions, assaults him with the rooster and great vehemence. The young man thus belabored grapples with his assailant and a hard struggle ensues, the attacked party finally getting hold of one leg of the now thoroughly demoralized chicken. A violent bracing apart, a sharp scuffle, and the chicken is torn in two. Loud are the cries of " Putz-eesh ! Putz-eesh ! " as the two now rush upon two others and begin walloping them with the sundered sides of the chicken. Time after time the bleeding flesh is forcibly subdivided by the excited contestants, and with each new piece the number of fighters is augmented. Some of the big fellows hand their gallinaceous clubs to the youngsters, until at last two chubby tots, not over three years old, are struggling like little wildcats over a bedraggled " drumstick." All around the blows are the hardest the dealers keep in stock, yet neither baster nor basted gets angry. On the contrary, both are laughing as long as they have breath ; and when at last the violent sport has worn itself out, the victors sit down and gnaw the dusty and well-macerated flesh, which is believed to have sovereign qualities.

By this time the sun is falling low toward the black *mesa*, and already some of the non-combatants are lassoing and saddling their horses from the *caballada.* Five-sixths of the men of the town, and two-thirds of the boys, are mounted, riding up and down the streets, and showing their paces to the women above.

Having paraded singly and in groups to their heart's content, the cavalcade, numbering one hundred and fifty horsemen, files out around the rear of the church and starts down the horse trail, or rather the ticklish stairway, down which Acoma horses stump unhesitatingly, though an Eastern horse would faint at the mere sight of it.

Down at the foot of one of the noble flanking buttes of sandstone the poles are again erected, with another chicken dangling between them, and on their spirited steeds these wild riders re-enact the chicken race.

The first house in town, as one comes up from the horse-trail, is the large *casa* of Martin, the fine old ex-Governor. Riding up to this the flushed riders wedge their horses in front, and with shouts of " *Tse-ai-tee-ah!* " lift three hundred hands to their highest. In a moment, from the door of the second-story emerge Martin's two buxom daughters, richly dressed, each bearing upon her head a heaping *jicara*. Setting their baskets down on the edge of the roof they begin to hurl the contents out upon the heads of the crowd. Pieces of gay-colored calico, quarters of jerked mutton, *tortillas*, and loaves of bread of a peculiar, sacred form go flying through the air amid the yells of the crowd. The deftness with which the men on horseback catch these missiles would secure them a first-class baseball engagement in the East, and the mysterious fashion in which they stow away what they secure would put Hermann to the blush. The dismounted ones run under the horses, unmindful of bronco hoofs, and grab whatever misses the clutches of the horsemen.

When a shower of gum-drops from the inverted baskets show that no more is to be expected there, the cavalcade gives a parting yell and rushes on to the next house, and so on throughout the whole town. Then the horses are returned to the crowd of their unridden fellows and the crowd breaks up. A little later one may see the Navajo squaws filling their blankets with the bushels of provisions they have captured, while the recent racers are riding through the *caballada* with little pitchers, from which they take generous mouthfuls of water and blow it over their favorite steeds — a sure safeguard against all equine ills.   Then, too, scores of tiny bare boys run along the houses, while the women pour water on them from above—another custom of medicinal authority.

The big, red moon peeps over the horizon, and finding the coast clear, comes climbing up.   The streets empty themselves upon the housetops.   As the hours slip by the chatting and chanting groups grow fewer.   Now and then a few young men come down the street dancing in stately measure, or wrestle on the patches of soft sand.   And when at last the shrunken moon looks down from behind the great church, all Acoma is asleep and the feast of the Beloved Disciple is over.

XI

THE CITIES THAT WERE FORGOTTEN

THE CITIES THAT WERE FORGOTTEN

THE most remarkable hiatus in American history —and perhaps in all history—is that which sunders the past and present of the Quivíra. Individuals have now and then lost identity; but never elsewhere was there a town so consummately confounded. Altogether gratuitously, but so fully that a century will scarce identify it to the slow world, it has become the Iron Mask of cities. Such gilded myths never hung so long before on one unshifting spot; and the Golden Fleece itself fathered less heroism and hardship, less disappointment and thirsty death. Probably a hundred Americans know of the Dorado of South America, to every one who ever heard of the Quivíra; but a strange ashen ruin in our own land has become the home of a myth as startling and as potent in history, as that which sprung from the yearly plunge of a gold-dusted cacique into Lake Puatavitá. The fable of the Quivíra it was which led to the first great interior exploration of what is now United States—eighty years before the Saxon had penetrated to a hundred miles from the Atlantic coast, and nearly three centuries before he got so far inland as were the Spanish chasers of the Quivíra—and it played an important part in the opening and colonization of the vast region between Kansas City and California. Three hundred

and fifty years ago it inspired an astounding march
which has never since been paralleled in North
America ; and to this day it has not ceased to count its
yearly victims.   And besides playing golden will-o'-
the-wisp through all that the world has been and
seen since good Queen Bess dropped pinafores, it
stands alone as the largest blunder of history—and
also as the stage of the Ultimate Folly.

The myth of the Quivíra, for centuries a vagabond,
sat down at last in one of the astounding ruins of the
Manzano Plains, one hundred and fifty miles south of
Santa Fé, and eighty southeast of Albuquerque.   If
those who fritter abroad, still ignorant of their own
land, with the plea " America is so new, and has no
ruins," might see the cities of the Accursed Lakes, they
would grow modest as to the castles of the Rhine.
And if our histories, which seem to fancy that America began with Jamestown and Plymouth Rock, might
imbibe somewhat of that eternal pursuit, that sleep-
less seeking, of which the Quivíra is one monument,
it would be the better for justice and for intelligence.

The birth and development of this most romantic
(and historically most important) of North American
myths, is so curious, and in one way so complicated,
that one scarce knows from which end to approach it
—whether from the terminus of cause or that of effect.
There are some reasons, however, which make it
seem best to trace the first half of this strange
double story chronologically.

The Quivíra myth was born in New Mexico in
1540, of poor and none too honest parents.   Its
father was an Indian captive ; its mother that drab,
Opportunity ; its nurse, who went bankrupt in the

A QUIVIRA MYTH-MAKER.

suckling, the most remarkable explorer that ever trod
North American soil.   And it all came to pass by
one of the most brilliant executive minds of the sixteenth century, that great first Viceroy of New Spain,
Antonio de Mendoza.

Generally speaking, the New World had already
been conquered by and for Spain.   There was still
an infinity to be done; but the broad foundations of
Spanish America had been laid—and in a cement
which time will never crumble.   Mexico was no
longer an empire to be fought for, but a province to
be developed; and the reaction after conquest means
always danger.   Already the young Spanish blades
there

> " For want of fighting had grown rusty,
> And ate into themselves for lack
> Of somebody to hew and hack."

Just as the rust grew menacing, came Fray Marcos's
discovery of New Mexico—and Mendoza saw his opportunity.   To the ambitious and already renowned
soldier Francisco Vasquez de Coronado, he gave an
expedition of these restive cavaliers, and strict orders
to take them hunting and never bring them back.

The first half of this command Coronado carried
out with a vengeance.   He led his fistful of an army
through the exploration of thousands of desert miles
within our own area that not one per cent. of present
Americans ever dreamed of.   His expeditions discovered the greatest chasm on earth—the Grand
Cañon of the Colorado—and most of the other
marvels of the Southwest, three centuries before a
Saxon ever saw any of them.   In the latter weeks of
1540 he had his quarters at the pueblo of Tiguex—

now the pretty town of Bernalillo—on the Rio Grande, in central New Mexico. Thence he made a reconnoissance to the pueblo of Pecos ; and there the myth was born.

It is a striking truth that in the whole opening of the two Americas fable was a far more important agent than fact ; and this was as marked in the area which is now ours as in the southern continent. The first of our present States to be entered by Caucasians, and the earliest town in our nation to be founded, were entered and founded under the lead of fairy-tales. As it was with Florida, so with the Southwest. Had it not been for the mythical broidering given the real " Seven Cities of Cibola," Mendoza would never have sent Coronado into New Mexico ; and but for sequel-myths, the greatest pathfinder would never have made his unparalleled march.

Disappointed, of course, in the fabled gold of the Seven Cities—which were merely Pueblo towns like Zuñi, their surviving child—Coronado was revolving the best way to carry out the second part of his orders, to colonize and stay. It chanced that the Pecos then had a captive Plains Indian—very probably a Pawnee—whom they had bought from the Apaches. This slave was notable among his longhaired Pueblo masters for the fashion in which his head was shaven—only the scalp-lock being left, after the custom of his people—and will go down history under the nickname the Spaniards gave him, of " the Turk." Whether he was sole progenitor of his disastrous offspring cannot be positively known ; but the presumption is strong that he had to father a creature

19

of his captors.   He had nothing to gain by the invention, but they a great deal—namely, to rid themselves of their unwelcome guests.

At all events it came to pass that " the Turk," apprised of the failure of the Spaniards to find that yellow stone they were seeking, informed Coronado that he wot where there was much.   Before he came to captivity and New Mexico, he knew a tribe of the plains which had great store of this substance.   The tribe was called Quivíra, and he could lead to its range.   No sooner said than attempted to be done. Coronado took his " army " and his guide, and went again rainbow-chasing.   The Turk led them east into the trackless plains, intending—as he afterward confessed—to lose them and let them perish in those appalling wastes.   But, like many a later confidence-man, he had attempted the wrong greenhorn.   At about the centre of our present Indian Territory, Coronado, finding that he was being duped and that the guide was leading them in a circle, sent back to Tiguex the bulk of his little force, and taking the lead himself, carried his thirty men through frightful hardships to very near where Kansas City now stands.   And here he found the Quivíras—but, I hardly need say, no gold.   There was in the whole tribe one solitary fragment of any metal—a bit of native copper worn on the necklace of a war captain. The Quivíra was a Teton nomad—a cousin of the Sioux—drifting with the buffalo, which was his politics and his profession ; planting a little corn when the bison stood still, leaving it when he wandered— a mere aboriginal Gypsy, without house or wealth or art.   It is all plain enough.   Every eye-witness who then or thereafter saw the Quivíras, describes them precisely as utter barbarians, clothed only in skins, eating raw meat, and having no bread, no metal, no towns, no arts whatever, " *una gente muy bestial, sin policia ninguna en las casas, ni en otra cosa.*" * And that was the reward of the most amazing expedition ever made on our soil !

Having thus broken the golden bubble of the Quivíra, and with it his own stout heart, Coronado beheaded the treacherous guide, and, with his little following, retraced his fearful way to Tiguex, where we must leave him.   But his having reduced it to an absurdity was not the end of the chimera.   It was too vigorous a youngster to perish of mere annihilation. Truth crushed to earth never rises again with half the agile alacrity of error ; and it was not half a century after Coronado had fully shown up the Quivíra swindle before it began to find other victims.   Even the hard-headed colonizer of New Mexico, the founder of the second and third Caucasian towns in all our country, Juan de Oñate, was not proof against the bright mirage, and chased it assiduously, but in vain.   And after him came many another—Alonzo Vaca, in 1634 ; and Governor Luis de Rozas, in 1638 ; and Diego de Guadalajara, about 1654 ; and Juan Dominguez de Mendoza, in 1684, and many before and many after— and many a one of them laid their bones to whiten along the thirsty trail of that elusive vision.   It has been for three hundred years the siren of the South-

---

* Relacion del Suceso, p. 326.   See also Coronado's Carta á su Magestad, 1541, p. 246 et seq.; Juan Jaramillo's Relacion Hecha, p. 315 ; Castañeda's Cibola, p. 194 ; Torquemada, Gomara, Herrera, and every other Spanish source bearing on this point.

west.   I know of but one thing so remarkable as that
so many Spaniards—so many college men as well as
soldiers of them—should have given ear to that golden
lie ; and that is, that a hundred times as many Americans trust it as implicitly to-day.

So much for the original myth of the Quivíra—a
wilful and treacherous falsehood, in the first place ;
and in the second, distinctly invented only for, and
applicable only to, a nomad tribe in northeastern Kansas ; and thirdly, nailed and pilloried as a lie in that
same year of its birth, 1540.   To trace the modern
perversion of what now becomes the Gran * Quivíra,
we will begin the other end-to.

South of Albuquerque, the chief commercial town
of the Territory, the narrow valley of the Rio Grande
is rimmed on the east by an arid plateau, twenty miles
wide ; and this in turn is walled by a long cordillera
of ten thousand foot peaks—the Sandia, the Bosque,
the Manzano, the Oscuro.   Climbing that rugged
barrier, or threading one of its passes, the traveller
thence descends through park-like pineries to the
edge of the infinite eastward plains.   In the centre of
his bare, brown vista gleams a chain of ghastly white
salines, the Accursed Lakes of Tigua folk-lore.   These
once were fresh—the story runs—the home of fish
and water-fowl, the drinking-places of the bison and
the antelope.   But in one of them dwelt an unfaithful
wife, and for her sins the lakes were accursed to be
salt forever.   Beyond them the dead plain melts upon
the indeterminate horizon.   Between them and the
cordilleras, dark, low ridges fade from pine-clad slope
to barren prairie.   Far southeast and south are the

* Great.

spectral peaks of the Sierra de la Gallina, the Sierra
Capitana, the Sierra del Carrizo, the Sierra Blanca;
and to the farther north the dim blue shadows of the
range of Santa Fé. It is a strange, weird outlook—a
visual leap into space. There is nothing else quite so
like it as the eastward view from the top of Pike's
Peak.

Along the smooth, timbered lower slope of the
Manzano is a north and south line of ancient Pueblo
ruins. The mounds of long-abandoned Shúmnac and
its sister towns bleach beside their squalid successors,
the Mexican plazas of Chililí, Tajíque, and Manzano.
A little farther south, and pointing a right-angled triangle, are the bones of the three chief cities of the
salines—Abó, Cuaráy, and Tabirá. It must be understood that I use the word "cities" here with a restric-
tion and not in the sense of the Romantic School.
These were cities like Montezuma's "capital," though
smaller. There was no hint of a metropolis—no
palaces, no temples, no splendor. Like those of en-
fabled Mexico, these towns were mere piles of earth
and stone—Pueblo communities exactly such as are
seen to-day in Taos, Acoma, Zuñi. None of them,
here or in Mexico, were entitled by size or magnifi-
cence to be called cities, and the term is applied to
them, simply because architecturally, socially, and
politically they were of an organization complete beyond what is expressed by our word "town." Each
was a self-governing, independent commonwealth,
compact and fortified; a republic within walls; and
as such they seem more fitly entitled "cities," with
due insistence upon the special limitations of the word
here.

Twenty miles south of the New Mexican hamlet of Manzano, and the riddle of its ancient apple-trees, is

ABO—THE WESTERN WALL.

the noble ruin of the pueblo of Abó.   Its site is a wee bead of a valley, strung upon a deep and ragged arroyo, between an eastern rocky ridge and the long acclivity to the mountains.   The pueblo itself was a large hollow square, over two hundred feet on a side, of unbroken, three-story stone houses, terraced toward, and opening upon, the safe inner court. Outside, and parallel with, the north end of this quadrangle was a separate block of three-story buildings. So far the ruins present nothing novel to the student of Pueblo antiquities. They are merely the usual tousled mounds of fallen building-stone and inblown sand. But a few rods north of the pueblo tower the giant walls of a noble edifice—such walls as would have been long ago immortalized in American literature, were they in Rhenish Bavaria instead of a land which might be fancied to have a patriotic interest to Americans. Amid the talus of tumbled stone these two vast parallel walls, forty-two feet apart, one hundred and fifteen feet long, and twelve feet thick at the base, soar sixty feet aloft in rugged majesty. Their ancient masonry of darkly-rufous sandstone, in adobe mortar, is almost perfect in alignment still. A spade slides smoothly down their plane surfaces. The two end walls of the structure are gone to utter wrack; and the one-time floor is lost under a dozen feet or more of their jumbled ruin. The long-potent Romantic School would have it, of course, that this was a temple of the Sun, and built of " dressed stone," as usual. It is as well to note, in passing, that there is no dressed stone in any ancient ruin of New Mexico or Arizona—though there are numberless handsome walls which the theorizer will (not altogether inexcusably) insist were wrought. But while the prehistoric aborigine here had no tools wherewith to dress any rock but tufa, the natural cleavage and the fractile lines of the sandstone were extremely

kind to him, and he could pick from his quarry ready-
made slabs which had every appearance of having
been roughly worked.

The wee oasis of Abó is not now a solitude, though
the tribe that builded its dark piles long ago faded
from off the face of the earth.   A half-dozen Mexican
families dwell under the gigantic cottonwoods that sap
the puny rill; and here is the home of the *paisano*
genius—immortalized in territorial proverb—who

" fué por Socorro, y no supo porqué."

He made the long and trying journey in safety; but
on arriving at Socorro knew not why, and had to return to Abó to ask his *comadre*, "For what went
I?"   This information gained, he trudged back his
fifty miles and fulfilled his mission, and trudged home
again.   His house, and all, are built of ready stone
from the huge dark walls that frown down upon the
degenerate present.

The second corner of the forgotten triangle is fifteen miles east of Abó, within rifle-shot of the Mexican townlet of Punta de Agua.   Here, in another
bowl-like little vale, with outlook between its rim-
ridges to the weary sea of prairie, crumble the reli-
quiæ of the ancient pueblo of Cuaraí.*   Like Abó, the
ruined city itself is a huddle of indeterminate mounds
of masonry, and less imposing than many longer-
abandoned pueblos.   But, like Abó too, it is compan-
ioned by a huge and mysterious edifice—an edifice in
ruins, it is true, but so tall, so solemn, so dominant of
that strange, lonely landscape, so out of place in that
land of adobe box-huts, as to be simply overpowering.

* Spelled also in the older MSS., Cuarác.

On the Rhine it would be a superlative; in the wilderness of the Manzano it is a miracle. Its great, shadowy walls are neither so lofty nor so thick as those of Abó; but neither are they so breached. The great rectangle is practically complete, with three walls largely perfect, and part of the fourth. The masonry is quite as fine as at Abó, and the architecture as imposing. A big modern chapel, a few ; ods to the

CUARAI FROM THE SOUTHWEST.

east, is built of plundered stone, but the ancient temple seems scarce to feel the robbery. Its roof long ago disappeared, but the massive walls stand firm as the mother ledges, and still hold the careful mortises for long-forgotten rafters. At the foot of the hillock is a tiny rivulet, sentinelled by a tall and lonely pine; and upon the hillside, a few hundred yards south, is a large, strange circular enclosure fenced about with upright slabs of rock.

The third and southeast corner of the triangle is thirty miles from Cuaraí, and about the same distance from Abó; much farther from the mountains than they, but hardly more in the plains—since it is in an outlying huddle of round ridges. The country here is much higher than on the western side of the cordillera—the pueblo which we now approach is 6,047

INTERIOR OF THE RUIN OF CUARAI.

feet above the sea-level. Access to it is difficult and dreary   The nearest water is thirty miles away ; and the explorer must carry not only provisions, but water for himself and animals. Toiling down the edge of the ghastly plains, thence into long, smooth trough-valleys, along the eastern acclivity of the dark-wooded Mesa de los Jumanos, ankle deep in the sands of the médano, the traveller feels at every step, with every breath, a crowding influence he knows not what.

Mid-ocean is not more lonesome than the plains, nor
night so gloomy as that dumb sunlight. It is barren
of sound. The brown grass is knee-deep—and even
that trifle gives a shock, in this hoof-obliterated land.
The bands of antelope that drift, like cloud shadows,
across the dun landscape suggest less of life than of
the supernatural. The spell of the plains is a wondrous thing. At first it fascinates. Then it bewilders.
At last, it crushes. It is sure as the grave and
worse. It is intangible but resistless ; stronger than
hope, reason, will—stronger than humanity. When
one cannot otherwise escape the plains, one takes
refuge in madness.

But on a sudden, the tension is relieved. A mile to
the south, where a whaleback ridge noses the uncanny
valley, stands out a strange ashen bulk that brings us
back to earth. Wan and weird as it is, it bespeaks
the one-time presence of man, for Nature has no such
squarenesses.

I do not believe that the whole world can show
elsewhere, nor that a Doré could dream into canvas,
a ghostliness so *à propos*. Stand upon the higher
ridges to the east, and it is all spread before you, a
wraith in pallid stone—the absolute ghost of a city.
Its ashen hues which seem to hover above the dead
grass, foiled by the sombre blotches of the junipers ;
its indeterminate gray hints, outspoken at last in the
huge, vague shape that looms in its centre ; its
strange, dim outlines rimmed with a flat, round world
of silence—but why try to tell that which has no telling ? Who shall wreak expression of that spectral
city ?

Come nearer, and the spell dwindles ; but it is

never broken. Even as we pass our hands over that forgotten masonry of pale limestones, or clamber over fallen walls with tangible stubbing of material toes, the unearthliness of the haggard scene does not wholly cease to assert itself. Only, we now know that it is not a ghost-city, which the next breeze may waft away. It is a ruined pueblo again—but such a pueblo! Not in size nor in architecture—there are several others as large, and some as imposing—but in color and in setting it is alone. Small wonder for the folly of its later devotees—it seems the rightful home of superstition, and here the wildest myth need not be ill at ease.

This was the pueblo of Tabirá, infinitely better known, in this day of grace and putative light, as the "Gran Quivíra." It was one of the larger pueblos of New Mexico, and in its day had perhaps fifteen hundred inhabitants; not more. It was a village of unusual shape, prescribed by the topography of the ridge; a long, narrow array of three and four story terraced houses in vaguely parallel blocks, facing each other across narrow alleys. Six circular estufas, partly subterranean, yawn at random amid the ruins. The walls of the houses have toppled to high rubbish mounds—hardly one stands to tell its former stature. Only a few rooms of first and second stories, long innocent of roofs, gape from out the moraine of time. But at the centre of the southerly blocks is still the gray, quadrangular wall—now sadly battered—of a very large building, with traces of an enclosure at its east end. And in the western terminus of the village, just on the brow of the slope that falls away to the strange valley and looks across to the sombre Mesa de los Jumanos, is another and a gigantic ruin, whose like is not in all our North America.   Its walls, thirty feet high and six feet thick, roofless and ragged at the

TABIRA—REAR ENTRANCE WITH CARVED LINTEL.

top, two hundred and two feet front and one hundred and thirty-one feet in greatest depth, are of the same spectral bluish-gray limestone, broken into irregular but flat-faced prisms and firmly laid in adobe mortar.

The northern part of this bewildering ruin is one huge cruciform room, thirty-eight feet wide and one hundred and thirty-one feet long, with an eastward gateway fifteen feet wide and eleven high, under a mighty timber which upholds fifteen feet of massive masonry. South of this enormous room is a honeycomb of chambers of ordinary size, divided by long halls, and with sides still standing to a height of twenty feet. Of these rooms there are a score. It is plain that they had no upper stories, as had the dwellings of the pueblo. There is also a rear entrance from the south to the great room, through a spacious ante-chamber. In one of the apartments of the honeycomb is still a perfect fireplace; and here and there over the vacant doorways are carved-wood lintels, their arabesques softened but not lost in the weathering of centuries. Some of the rafters must have weighed a ton and a half to two tons; and the trees which gave them were at least fifteen miles away.

Here is the asylum of the modern Quivíra-myth; the Mecca of the Southwestern fortune-hunter; the field of the Last Folly. That it should have been chosen from among all the fifteen hundred pueblo ruins in New Mexico for credulity to butt its head against, is not strange physically. Its bleak, unearthly site, the necromancy of the plains, its ghostly aspect, and its distance from all water, were enough to stop and hold the later treasure-seekers, who had heard vaguely that "Coronado hunted the Quivíra," but utterly failed to hear that he found it—found it in northeastern Kansas, and found it worthless. These new victims found this unprecedented ruin of Tabirá a century ago; and to them we owe the misnomer

of Gran Quivíra. Since their day its rest has been
yearly broken. At first were those who pried in the
débris-choked lower rooms of the pueblo, and gophered under the mighty walls of the temple. But
they were only poor *paisanos* who could neither read
nor ask of history. Within the last decade members
of the Superior Race drilled down through a hundred
feet of the eternal bedrock in quest of *buried* treasure,
and the ruins of Tabirá are so peppered with their
shafts that it is unsafe to move about by night.

For the myth of the Quivíra has come to Tabirá to
stay. Neither fact nor reason will ever fully dislodge
it, and it will always count its dupes. It has even
grown, in that arid home, to startling proportions.
The Quivíra of Coronado is forgotten, and in its stead
is the Gran Quivíra. It is no resurrection of the
old myth, but the invention of a new. To keep in it
the vital spark its nurses have to stand history upon
its head, and turn the compass inside out; to give
the lie to the sober record of eye-witnesses, and the
ear to professional myth-makers. Scarce a month
goes by in which the territorial newspapers do not
print some new fable or allusion to the old; and even
as I write, an expedition is fitting out in Albuquerque
to seek "the buried treasure." The folk-lore of the
Mexican population has suddenly become exuberant
with new Quivíra tales. Every now and then an
awe-struck shepherd staggers in under a new version.
He has leaned against a great bowlder, which forthwith slid in its carved grooves and disclosed a subterranean passage, whose farther darkness was aflame
with jewels and yellow ingots. Or a huge white
snake has risen from the ground at midnight to show

him the *locus* of the treasure; or a spectral goat led him; or he has heard, just at high noon, the roar of a great subterranean river. *Et id fabularum genus omne.* The superior prospector, besides swallowing

TABIRA—MAIN ENTRANCE TO THE GREAT HALL.

all this, has improved upon it by adding a " dying confession " and cipher manuscripts, and mystic maps that "have come down from the old days." There has even been in the Territory, for nearly a generation, a standing reward of $10,000 to him who should discover the lost water of Gran Quivíra.

This second edition of the Quivíra myth is not at

first sight so remarkable. It seems merely the wonted accretion of fable around the mysterious. It is only when we turn to history that we can conceive the full folly of this perversion—the bewildering blunder of the Cities that were Forgotten. For they once were *so* well known ! There is no mystery about them—as well should a Hottentot explorer make a mystery of Bunker Hill. They are as stable in history as Plymouth Rock. And above all, they have no remotest kinship with the Quivíra. That was eight hundred miles northeast of them. That was an errant village of tepees—these, fortified towns of immemorial stone. That was always Quivíra ; these were always Abó, Cuaraí, and Tabirá. About the only point of resemblance was that neither had ever a particle of gold or of any other treasure whatever. No one ever confounded the two until long after the world was old enough to know better. The ruins are Pueblo ruins, as a matter of course ; and as a matter of history they are ruins of the Tompíros Pueblos, a branch of the now extinct Píro stock. The first Caucasian to penetrate the country of the Accursed Lakes was Francisco Sanchez de Chamuscado, who discovered these then living towns in 1581, and set them in history. A year later came Espejo, who also saw and described these pueblos—which Chamuscado noted as the best towns he had yet found. In 1598 Juan de Oñate, the first governor of New Mexico, paid his official visit to these cities of the salines, and received the formal submission of their people to the Crown of Spain. The usual humane and comprehensive Spanish policy reached as well the pueblos of the plains as those of the Rio Grande. Statecraft exhaustively studied their material, the Church their spiritual, needs. On September 9, 1598—twenty-two years before the Mayflower—a priest was assigned to these three cities, and their numerous neighbor pueblos. This was Fray Francisco de San Miguel, one of the chaplains of Oñate's little army. His station was at Pecos (a pueblo deserted in 1840), whence he had to administer his enormous parish to the south. That the size of his circuit did not hinder his missionary success, nor that of those who came after, is written not only in the conversion of those wild tribes to Christianity, but also in undecaying stone. For the huge and mysterious ruins at Abó, Cuaraí, and Tabirá were merely Christian churches, built by the Pueblos under the patient guidance of the Franciscan fathers, and with the aid of Spanish tools. The mission of Tabirá was founded by the fraile Francisco de Acevedo, in or about 1628 ; * and the smaller church was built soon after. In time its needs outgrew it ; and some time after the death of Fray Acevedo, in 1644, the enormous newer church and " convent " were erected. It seems to have been designed to make Tabirá a central mission ; and accommodations were provided for the residence of a considerable number of priests. But these huge edifices were never fully finished. The churches of Abó and Cuaraí were erected under the same régime and at about the same time ; all three aboriginal cities were as much a part of Spanish missionary work and Spanish history as was Santa Fé itself. The civil legislation for their benefit, the slow, sure uplifting of those savage flocks by their gentle Franciscan teachers, is

* Vetancurt . Menologio, p. 260, etc.

not unrecorded—from Fray de San Miguel down through the resident missionaries, Fray Francisco Letrado, Fray Acevedo, Fray Juan de Zalas, beloved Fray Geronimo de la Llana, and all that heroic list. There were no fairy-tales about the Manzano pueblos then—nor long thereafter. So late as the latter half of the last century an official map of New Mexico marked the ruined pueblo of Tabirá in its proper place—the place since usurped, in popular superstition, by the Gran Quivíra.

That these cities so suddenly disappeared from the world's knowledge, we have to thank not only the world's carelessness, but also that red history-maker, the Apache. This scourge of the plains was always particularly attentive to the exposed cities of the salines—which had more pregnable locations than the usual Pueblo fort-town—and at last overthrew them. The exact date is not sure, but it was positively between 1670 and 1675. It was a period of his goriest activity. In 1672 he made the massacre of Há-ui-cu, one of the Zuñi towns, two hundred miles west. In 1675 he wiped out the New Mexican pueblo of Senecú (on the Rio Grande, where San Antonio now stands) killing Fray Alonzo Gil de Avila and many of his flock. And between these two grim entries he wrote his crimson autograph across the six chief towns of the Manzano plains—the Tigua pueblos of Chililí, Tajíque, and Cuaraí, and the Píro pueblos of Jumancas, Abó, and Tabirá.* The scant survivors of the latter towns fled to El Paso, and their score or so of descendants, who live to-day at Senecú, in Chihua-

---

* Vide Fray Juan Alvarez, MS. Carta ; Fray Silvestre Velez de Escalante, Carta al Padre Morfí, and other undisputed sources.

hua, are all that is left of the once potent Píro stock. Those who escaped death at Cuaraí, being Tiguas, fled to their brethren at Shee-e-huíb-bac, now Isleta, whose fathers all had come, according to their traditions, from other Apache-erased pueblos of the Manzano plain. Even the Jumanos—those strange neighbor " Rayados," who were unique in the Southwest by their fashion of tatooing or slashing their

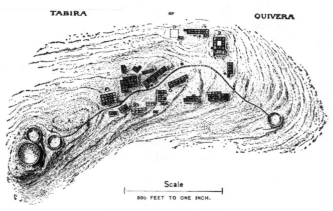

GROUND PLAN OF TABIRA.
A, A, A, A, tanks ; B, large church and convent ; C, old church ; D, cemetery ; S, S, S, ancient acequia.

faces—were swept off by that same merciless besom. With 1675 the last germ of aboriginal life had vanished from that once populous era. For a century the plain was utter desert and in the undisputed clutch of the Apache ; and only the huge vetebræ of those dead cities bleached in glaring sun and savage snows. At last the Mexican post-pioneer crept in ; and now a few hundreds of his children are scattered along that vast solitude. The fence of an enormous American cattle-rancho stretches almost to Tabirá. But it was too late for the fallen cities. Already they were forgotten ; and the unread new neighbors, instead of rehabilitating that heroic past, served but to distort it to an ignoble if romantic caricature. That zeal which made Christian conquest, without arms, of this savage wilderness, has fared as ill with the myths, as have its monuments with the facts, of latter days. The one has been "borrowed" to frame a Captain Kidd fable ; the other to build goat-corrals.

Of the three great churches, that of Cuaraí is largest, having a floor-area of 5,020 square feet. That of Tabirá comes next, with 4,978 square feet ; and then Abó, with 4,830. These figures are for the auditoriums alone, and do not include the extensive "convents" attached to each, of which that at Tabirá is most extensive, covering 13,377 square feet. The walls of Abó are much the noblest and most massive, and those of Tabirá the crudest, though no less solid. The pueblos of Abó and Cuaraí had each a tiny but sufficient rill ; but Tabirá is absolutely dry. There is neither spring nor stream in thirty miles. But this is hardly a rare thing among Pueblo ruins ; and it is well known that the aborigines were wont to "kill" their water when forced to abandon a town, lest it give comfort to the enemy. We know, not only by record, but by eyesight, of several cases where, with infinite labor, the Pueblos actually obliterated a spring to keep it from their savage neighbors. But this though a probable, is not an essential, factor in the problem. On the brow of the acclivity east of Tabirá—and connected with it by a still traceable ditch—are three large reservoirs of earth, rudely rimmed with stone, to catch and hold the rain and snow. This was the waterworks of Tabirá, and an adequate system. The

Píros had no animals, unless a few sheep and horses
already derived from the Spaniards ; and their crops
of corn, beans, and squashes grew then as now, by
the annual precipitation and without need of irrigating.   The reservoirs were ample for their duty—to
supply water for domestic use.   It is entirely possible
that there was also a near spring which was plugged
at the downfall of Tabirá ; and the least crazy of the
prospectors who still throw away their means and
sometimes their lives there, are those that seek the
water which would make available a great range of
such pasturage as is now almost unknown in New
Mexico.

Such, in brief, are the cities of the salines—the
Cities that Were.   Prominent and clear figures in the
earliest history of our land, definite and mythless as
Hoboken, they suddenly dropped into popular obliv-
ion.   Their identity seemed as lost as though they
had never been ; and when their resurrection came
it was not to be remembered but recreated—not
rediscovered but invented.   For a century their
weary bones have been made to masquerade in a romantic mummery which would be laughable had it
not been the closing tragedy of so many lives.   It is
only within a decade that the light of record and common sense has been turned upon them, and that Bandelier's conclusive researches have laid forever the
myth of the Gran Quivíra and brought back to the
memory of history the cities that were so long forgotten.